Praise for *App Empire*

"Five months ago, I started making iPhone apps and was generating about $25 per day. Then I met Chad. Chad taught me that marketing in the app store differs from every other medium in the world. It's absolutely nothing like advertising in newspapers, radio, or online. Using the techniques Chad told me in just one meeting put me in the top 20 of the app store multiple times. I often have days where I break $2,000 profit and more. This is a book you don't want to put on the shelf. Read this from beginning to end as it has simple secrets that are making people millions."

—Trey Smith, Underground Marketer
and iPhone Game Developer

"Chad has radically changed the game again. He is insightful but challenges the status quo in the mobile app space. His proven system breaks down the daunting tasks of researching and creating apps all the way through to marketing and monetization. *App Empire* is a must-read for anyone in the app game or anyone who wants to quit his or her nine-to-five for a long-term sustainable business. And not just any business. A business where you have the flexibility to work from anywhere, pick your own hours, and have higher margins than almost any other business."

—Amish Shah, World Renowned Marketing Expert,
Co-founder of Digispace, an *Inc.* 500 company of 2010

"Chad is a total gangster when it comes to iPhone apps. The money he has made in such a short time is astonishing."

—Frank Kern, Highest-Paid Internet
Marketing Consultant in the World

"Make millions with apps while traveling all over the world? Well, there is a book for that, and you're holding it in your hands. I've seen first hand the amazing results Chad's strategies can produce in the App Store. Seize this opportunity to become a top appreneur and join the growing ranks of the new rich."

—Tayfun Karadeniz,
Leading iPhone App Monetization Gangster

"The strategies for making money with apps detailed in this book are proven, effective, and simple. There are very few people in the app space equipped to author this book, and Chad is one of them based on his repeated success from the beginning. The market for apps is still in its infancy so my best advice is to read the book and execute. Chad has made it easy for you."

—Alan Johanson, App Publisher, 18m
App Downloads, 11 Apps in Top Overall

"It's not just about having an idea. It's about executing it. As the app market grows, it's getting harder to gain visibility, and visibility is the key to success. This book breaks down the process into understandable concepts. It guides you step by step in executing the most efficient way to gain that visibility you need. Chad has it down to a science."

—Michael Moon from Free the Apps!
Top App Company and App Millionaire

"If you are getting started in appreneurship, Chad Mureta is your perfect personal trainer. This is a book that teaches you how to make millions of dollars in apps. Chad shares his mistakes and successes on these highly guarded secrets. He guides you to focus on the things that make millions of dollars rather than leaving it to luck. Often, developers like myself forget the reasons and bury our heads in app building. Chad's methodology will lead you to the lifestyle you dream about."

—Bess Ho, Mobile Architect at Archimedes Ventures, Book
Author, and iOS Instructor at Udemy

"Chad is the classic example of the American Dream. I'm fortunate to know Chad from the start of his wild app success. A regular guy with an exceptional plan. His formula for app success is scientific and repeatable by anyone. His down-to-earth style and earnest love of helping others makes for an understandable method that produces results fast. I've created my wealth and success through years of overworking and stress. Please save yourself the time, the energy, and the stress and follow Chad's simple app plan today."

—Joe Barresi, Entrepreneur, Owner of Several Manufacturing
Companies and Recently Added App Business

EMPIRE

EMPIRE

MAKE MONEY, HAVE A LIFE, AND LET TECHNOLOGY WORK FOR YOU

CHAD MURETA

WILEY

John Wiley & Sons, Inc.

Published by John Wiley & Sons, Inc., Hoboken, New Jersey.
Published simultaneously in Canada.

For general information on our other products and services or for technical support, please contact our Customer Care Department within the United States at (800) 762-2974, outside the United States at (317) 572-3993 or fax (317) 572-4002.

Wiley publishes in a variety of print and electronic formats and by print-on-demand. Some material included with standard print versions of this book may not be included in e-books or in print-on-demand. If this book refers to media such as a CD or DVD that is not included in the version you purchased, you may download this material at http://booksupport.wiley.com. For more information about Wiley products, visit www.wiley.com.

ISBN 978–1–118–10787–4 (cloth); ISBN 978–1–118–21680–4 (ebk);
ISBN 978–1–118–21694–1 (ebk); ISBN 978–1–118–21704–7 (ebk)

Printed in the United States of America.

10 9 8 7 6 5 4 3 2 1

I dedicate this book to every student of life who consistently dances in the face of fear, who pushes through obstacles with unyielding certainty, who has unrealistic dreams and pursues them against all odds, and, as President Theodore Roosevelt once put it, "Whose place shall never be with those timid souls who know neither victory nor defeat."

I am humbled by the opportunity to inspire you in your own journey to connect the dots.

Contents

Introduction
How I Accidentally Became an
App Millionaire

THE HAPPIEST PEOPLE ON EARTH

I spent some of the happiest days of my life sleeping on dirt and foraging for food. I hiked through rainforests and saw hidden waterfalls. I hunted wild boar alongside the villagers, and I toasted the tribe's 97-year-old chief with a bitter tonic called *kava kava*, which we drank from coconut shells.

I was on the island of Savusavu, one of the remotest of 336 islands along Fiji's archipelago. The people there laughed easily, ate simply, and lived off the earth. The island was made up of vibrant green mountains that shot up out of the pristine turquoise waters of the South Pacific.

I chose to spend a week living amongst the villagers there because they are considered to be some of the happiest people on earth. The people of the

Savusavu villages seemed about as content and satisfied as one could get, and though their ways puzzled me at times, their smiles didn't lie.

It was refreshing to see how the Fijian people lived, which differed from anything I had ever experienced before. What I learned from this culture in such a short time can be summed up in seven words: Less is more, and love is everywhere.

After leaving the village, I was so inspired that I wanted others to share the experience with me. To my surprise, I found a WiFi signal in a remote shop on the island, and I e-mailed two of my buddies, Patrick and Nadim, to join me. Being spontaneous by nature, Patrick jumped on a plane from South Carolina, and Nadim took the next plane from Bangladesh.

Two days later, we were sitting on the beach, soaking up the sun and the island's natural beauty.

"Hey, what should we do next?" asked Nadim.

"Well, I've always wanted to learn to scuba dive," I said. "I've never done that before."

"Yeah, that's it," he said.

I did a Google search on my iPhone and found a place on the island that offered scuba diving lessons. The Google Maps function showed it was across the street. We found a tiny shack near the rocky beach with a sign across the doorway that read "Diving lessons." Inside, a thin man with missing teeth and a huge grin said he would teach us to scuba dive and take us out in the water.

Two hours later, we were submerged 40 feet down, swimming in the purplish-blue ocean with a rainbow of fish and coral beneath us and huge, four-foot-long turtles beside us. Breathtaking . . . literally.

THE APPRENEUR LIFESTYLE

My life is about doing what I love while earning easy income. I run my business from my iPhone. I work in a virtual world, earning real dollars. I've hiked Ayers Rock in the Australian Outback, trekked with Aborigines across the desert, hiked the Rocky Mountains, got certified in solo skydiving, heli-skied in Whistler, Canada, saw my favorite team play in the NBA finals from courtside seats, walked on fire, went bungee jumping, and most important of all, learned not to take life so seriously.

For my next adventure, I plan to spend three months at a time in nine places I have always wanted to visit. This includes learning martial arts in Buenos Aires, Argentina; dancing salsa in Bogotá, Colombia; running with the bulls in Pamplona, Spain; and riding gondolas on the canals of Venice, Italy.

I have an amazing life and the truth is anyone can have this lifestyle regardless of his or her background. I am part of a growing community of appreneurs, entrepreneurs who make money from applications, or apps, that are used on smartphones like iPhones and Droids, and other mobile devices such as iPads or iPod Touches. Appreneurs can live anywhere and can start a business regardless of their stage in life. As of this writing, the world's youngest appreneur is nine, and the oldest is 80.

Appreneurs earn money, while creating lifestyles of great freedom. Two of my appreneur friends spend several months of the year doing nonprofit work in Vietnam, while their businesses are generating seven-figure incomes. Another is taking his kids to see the Seven Wonders of the World, creating priceless memories with his family. Still another friend goes backpacking throughout Europe with his wife for most of the year.

No matter what your dream lifestyle is, you can have it as an appreneur. You don't have to be versed in computer programming to do this.

When I started, I didn't have a clue about programming languages or how to write code. I still don't, but I was motivated to succeed at this business.

Due to my unique circumstances at the time, failing wasn't an option.

STARTING FROM A HOSPITAL BED

When you are on your deathbed, will you be able to say you lived a fulfilled life?

I nearly couldn't.

I started this business from a hospital bed, wondering if I even wanted to live. I had survived a terrible car accident that shattered my left arm. I had gone through two groundbreaking operations, and spent 18 months in painful rehabilitation.

With limited insurance, I had racked up $100,000 in medical bills. Even though I survived, I had no clue how to get out of the deep hole I felt trapped in.

Up until that point, I had worked for and started several companies and ultimately failed because I had burned myself out. My last business was a real estate franchise I started right before the real estate bubble burst.

Yes, my timing was exquisite.

Even as my own boss, I was tired of working 18-hour days without freedom. I wasn't an employee. I was a slave to my own business with all the pressure and responsibility. So, it was much worse.

The doctors put my arm back together with a titanium rod holding things in place from my elbow to my shoulder. It was an agonizingly painful ordeal but a huge wake-up call that I realize I was lucky enough to receive. After that, I made the decision that my old way of going through the motions of life would not do anymore. I had to find a way to live a life I could look back on without regret.

After my accident, I was moved to a physical rehabilitation center and worked on reconstructing my body, my mind, and ultimately my life. While rehabilitating, the books of thought pioneers like Anthony Robbins, author of *Unlimited Power*, strengthened my mind, and Timothy Ferris, author of *The 4-Hour Workweek*, inspired me with the idea of lifestyle freedom.

During that time, my good friend and future business partner, Tayfun, gave me an article about appreneurs and told me I should get into the business. I learned that most appreneurs were one- or two-person teams, with low costs, and the successful ones were bringing in millions in profits. Still in my hospital bed, I drew app ideas while taking intense pain medication.

Three weeks after my last surgery, desperate, broke, and grasping at straws, I borrowed $1,800 from my stepdad and jumped with both feet into the app business. The result?

In just over two years, I created and sold three app companies and made millions. Two months after launching my company, one of my apps averaged $30,000 a month cash flow. Later, the company's income reached $120,000 in one month. In all, I've developed more than 40 apps and have had more than 35 million app downloads across the globe. Over 90 percent of my apps were successful and have made money.

To this day, I still don't know how to upload or update apps. I outsource that work to programmers and let Apple do the distribution. I focus on monitoring trends and doing creative work while leading my company. Although I concentrate on Apple's iPhone apps in my business, most concepts I show you can be applied to other platforms, including Google Android and BlackBerry.

Every morning when I wake up, I lie in bed for an hour, viewing reports on my iPhone. After that, I go for a run and eat breakfast, I take another hour to outsource tasks, and I spend the rest of the day living an incredible life.

GAME PLAN

My success came from having a game plan.

Even though I work a few hours a day, I want to build an empire that will last for years to come. To do that, I developed core areas of my business I can monitor daily, weekly, and monthly. I call this core the seven pillars of an app business. Understanding these pillars will turn your business from a one-time lottery winner to an unlimited gold mine.

The chapters in this book are set up in a modular fashion, so if you need marketing ideas, reread the marketing chapter and so on. The ideas I share will help at every stage of growth, from launch to expansion. Sure, you can find answers to specific questions, but I suggest learning the overall game plan first because this will bring you long-term riches.

Each chapter ends with actions for you to take. You can use these while building your business to ensure you stay on track every step of the way. You can also find additional helpful resources at www.AppEmpire.com/resources.

THE REAL QUESTION

Why wouldn't you get into the app space now? Mobile technology isn't going away, and the industry is exploding worldwide. Look around and see how many people use their mobile phones to find a restaurant, text friends, or update their status on Facebook. This hot industry is only getting started. It's the perfect time to jump into the mobile game.

You can run your own app business because you don't need a lot of money, skill, or knowledge to begin. All you need is a mobile phone and a desire to succeed. This industry allows you the freedom to work from anywhere and to earn a paycheck to support it. Plus, the best part, is it's fun.

In this book, I give you the roadmap to riches in the app business. Whether you are a total novice or an experienced developer, I guide you in building a business that supports the lifestyle you want while growing your bank account year after year.

I'll share with you how to:

- Tune your mind for success.
- Make insane amounts of money, while working part-time.
- Outsource nearly everything, so you can enjoy your lifestyle.
- Work with people who can do the technology side of things, so you don't have to.
- Make your product crazy attractive, so people love to give you money.
- Partner with others who can double and triple your profits.
- Create a sustainable app business.
- Live life on your terms.

This is a time in history when technology has given us the tools to live as we want. All you need is the desire and a game plan. No matter your background, gender, race, education, or situation, you can build an app empire, while you are living the life you deserve.

You don't have to wait till someday to fulfill your dreams. You can start today.

The Treasure in Your Hand

Why Mobile Apps Can Make You Rich

Change is the law of life. And those who look only to the past or present are certain to miss the future.

—John F. Kennedy

After I sold my first app business, on a whim, I packed my bags, went to the airport, and jumped on the next plane that was leaving. I'm glad I brought a pillow because I ended up in Sydney, Australia. With time to spare and no set plans, I decided to hang out Down Under for the next five weeks and experience the place I had always dreamed of visiting.

The harbor in Sydney is stunningly beautiful—filled with the white sails of sailboats, deep blue water, clear sky, and a buzz of great people. The sound of gulls fills the air, and brightly colored street markets and vendors line the shore.

Walking along the harbor with the sun on my face, I remembered that during my spontaneous moment I hadn't told anyone where I was going. I wanted to surprise my mom by sharing this experience with her, so I called her using the Skype app on my iPhone. The video phone call showed my face with the harbor in the background.

"Where are you?" she asked, not recognizing the backdrop.

"Sydney," I said.

She had a perplexed look on her face and paused for about 20 seconds in silence.

"Australia?"

It blew her away. It blew me away that she was able to see the view and enjoy it with me. It was amazing to be able to share that moment, and it was even more special because that wouldn't have been possible a year earlier.

I use my iPhone for everything: to find restaurants, manage my employees, or look at my apps' daily stats and rankings. I can order a shrimp burrito from my phone, put in my credit card info, and go pick it up or have it delivered. I can have yoga lessons on my iPhone without going to a yoga class. I can stand in line at an airport and with a push of a button find out how much my business earned that day.

If used properly, the virtual world can be a potent tool to simplify and improve every aspect of your life.

As this virtual world evolves, people expect to have access to lots of things more quickly and easily. Consumer demands are changing because we can do more on our phones, and they are always in our pocket traveling with us wherever we go.

We have apps that can control cars, allow us to play the piano, teach languages, and even recognize songs and name the artists. Apps are vital assets that streamline information, enhancing our lives while educating and entertaining us. With apps, it's all about convenience, convenience, convenience.

Apps are changing the way we communicate and relay information, allowing us to connect with people from Cape Town in South Africa to Montreal in Canada to Shanghai in China. Everywhere!

You have to understand this about the app business: At the core, it's about how consumers are using this technology to connect with the world. The more you are aware of this, the more money you can make with apps.

But how fast is this industry growing? Will it last? Who are the biggest players? What are the trends? In this chapter, you will gain essential insights into the industry, which will serve as the foundation of your successful app business.

A BIGGER OPPORTUNITY THAN THE INTERNET!

Newsflash: Mobile technology is the next big thing, and it's still in its infancy, growing rapidly every day. It's causing an information revolution and creating a new age where everyone is connected. Even in places like Africa, many people who don't have the means to own computers are bypassing them and using smartphones instead. In Egypt, social media posts from cell phones contributed to the revolution that brought down President Hosni Mubarak.

More than 4.6 billion cell phones are being used worldwide, enough for two-thirds of the people on Earth. This is a global market and it's growing at an unprecedented pace. (See Figure 1.1.)

The app industry exists entirely on the Internet with no physical presence necessary, making it easy to do business from anywhere in the world. What about the Internet? This is the new Internet, transforming the way we transmit and assimilate information, opening doors to a new way of making money. It is the fastest growing industry in history and shows no signs of slowing down.

As you've heard before, timing is everything. The mobile industry is in its early stages, as the Internet was in 1997. People who saw the opportunity then, jumped in and made bucket-loads of money. In fact, those

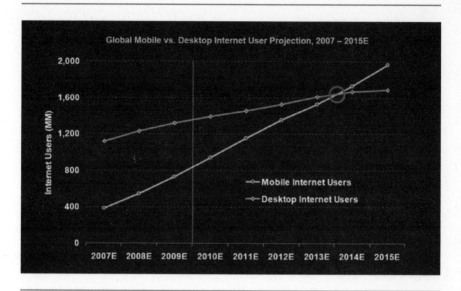

FIGURE 1.1   By 2014, mobile Internet will be used more than desktop Internet.

people are still making money because they have more experience and a competitive advantage over most.

Back in the early days, the Internet offered many new and easy ways to make lots of money. People were buying domain names for peanuts and selling them for millions. They were creating useful websites and selling advertising. A few websites, like Google and eBay, became integral parts of our lives and made their creators multi-billionaires. Years later, people are still making money from the Internet. The longer people waited to jump into the Internet money-making game, the more difficult it became.

What happened with websites is exactly what's happening now with apps and mobile technology. The only difference is that we have experienced the rise of the Internet and are conditioned to react more quickly to the app revolution. This means that the app world is running light-years ahead of the Internet, when it was at the same development stage. Developing apps is a chance to jump ahead of the masses and not be left behind, saying years from now, "I wish I had. . . ."

The numbers are off the charts. According to the technology research firm Gartner, Inc., total worldwide mobile app revenue is expected to explode to $58 billion by 2014. With more than 500,000 apps in the Apple app store, this industry is going to keep growing. There's no limit to the number of new apps that could be created because of our constant desire to be entertained or do more work with less effort. This demand will continue to be fueled by our society's hardwired need to evolve and grow.

Even with the recent global economic downturn, the app industry continues to grow. Many market researchers predict the mobile industry will continue to soar, but I'm not going to bog you down with more numbers. I will say that if you start now, you will be way ahead of the game. If you start later, you will still have plenty of opportunities, but why wait to live the lifestyle you can have today?

Another beautiful thing about this business is that you can start out part-time and go full-time later. That's how Lynn Duke started Fossil Software, one of the top app companies in the App Store. The company was born from the concept of bundling multiple, simple apps into one. He and his buddy, Marshall Womack, a designer, were working 80 hours a week at a gaming company. Their friend sent them an article about a guy who made $250,000 in a month from a simple app.

Lynn was unhappy, gaining weight, working overtime and tired of his long days. So, he worked with Marshall during nights and weekends over four months, while putting in lots of hours in their day jobs, to create their first app. Instead of creating one app, they decided to create 50 different apps and bundled them all into one app they called AppZilla. Fifty apps for the price of one. Now that's a deal. They had more than 60,000 downloads in the first month and that was just the beginning. Lynn quit his day job three weeks later, and they have been making loads of money and having a blast ever since.

LUDICROUS SPEED

In the movie *Spaceballs*, Colonel Sandurz and Dark Helmet have to steer their space ship faster than the speed of light. It's called ludicrous speed. That's what I think is happening in the app business. Technology is moving at ludicrous speed.

If you think about it, all the major change in human history has come with shifts in technology. When humans invented the wheel, life changed. When they created the steam engine and the cotton gin, the industrial revolution kicked off. When the World Wide Web became popular, we entered the Information Age. People could instantaneously connect and communicate with the rest of the world from their home or office. Now we carry the power of the Internet in our pockets and can call and text people any time from anywhere. Our lives are truly moving at ludicrous speed. Strap yourself in and enjoy the ride.

MOBILE APP TRENDS

These numbers from 148Apps.biz show how many apps are out there and how they're being used. I'm sure these numbers will be dwarfed quickly.

Apple App Store Stats Summary (January 2012)

Count of Active Applications in the App Store

Total Active Apps (currently available for download): 556,793
Total Inactive Apps (no longer available for download): 156,412
Total Apps Seen in U.S. App Store: 713,205
Number of Active Developers in the U.S. App Store: 132,604

Application Approval Delay

Maximum delay: 41 days
Average delay: 5.26 days

Application Price Distribution

Current Average App Price: $2.10
Current Average Game Price: $0.99
Current Average Overall Price: $1.95

Application Category Distribution (Most Popular Categories)

1. Games (96,187 active)
2. Books (60,707 active)
3. Entertainment (57,351 active)
4. Education (53,819 active)
5. Lifestyle (45,286 active)

Here are some more mind-blowing stats:

- Apple hit the 15-billion app download mark in three years—it took Apple over 7 years to sell 15 billion songs through iTunes.

- According to a study commissioned by mobile application store operator, GetJar, the mobile application market will reach $17.5B by 2012.
- Canalys is forecasting growth of $37B by 2015. Apple reports that iOS app developers have collectively made more than $3 billion in revenues since the App Store opened.
- Google's Android market, a rival platform and operating system to Apple's iPhone, hit 250,000 apps with more than 6 billion total downloads in mid-2011.
- On average, over 60 apps have been downloaded for every iOS device sold, according to market research firm Asymco.
- More than 30 million apps are downloaded every day, according to Asymco.
- The average selling price of paid apps will rise 14 percent year after year according to estimates by Piper Jaffray research firm and as reported in the *Wall Street Journal*.
- Apple expects to make more money on apps than on music by 2014 according to Asymco.

TAKE ADVANTAGE OF THIS PHENOMENON NOW

When I was first getting started, I didn't know about these business trends. I was excited to learn about entrepreneurs who had no previous experience in this business but were making money and enjoying freedom. It made sense to me. I had missed the Internet boom, and I wasn't about to miss this one, so I jumped in. Because of that, I can say that this is my time and it can be your time too.

This is the best time to launch into this business and take advantage of such an incredible opportunity.

Mobile technology is fun, exciting, and filled with possibilities. It isn't just a virtual reality. Instead, it's a business reality for anyone who is open and dedicated to making it work.

That being said, I will add one important distinction about the app business. People think that if they have one app idea, they can win the app lottery. The app business isn't about getting rich quickly with one app. It's about research, creativity, timing, and sound business sense, which includes creating several products instead of only one.

THE PLAYERS

Apps live on smartphones, just as various software programs live on computers. In smartphones, you can find several kinds of operating systems, called platforms. These platforms compete with each other for dominance in the smartphone market.

The three biggest players offering different platforms are Apple (iOS), Google (Android), and RIM (BlackBerry). Some app developers create products for all three platforms. Others specialize in one.

Focusing on creating apps for Apple's platform is the easiest way to make money in the app business because Apple dominates the app market and because it's easier to create apps for their devices. Apple devices all come with standard resolutions and compatible hardware, and there is only one mobile store for iOS apps. In contrast, Google's Android has different phones with different screen sizes and multiple app stores. This makes developers' lives harder and more complicated. They have to do additional programming for each Android device. It's a hassle and costs you more. You can focus on creating more apps and more successful apps when you don't have to spend time adapting your apps to all the different devices.

Consumers trust Apple's brand, and they have strong loyalty to Apple's line-up of iOS devices. The company is known for its intuitive and innovative products, and the brand continually grows stronger with its cult-like following.

So, start with the easiest, most well-known platform. Once you master that and gain more confidence, move to the other platforms and master those.

Table 1.1 shows the platforms in this app market.

Even though Apple is my preference and leads the industry, more platforms mean more consumers are downloading apps. The new markets are expanding and may be fertile ground as you grow in your app business. While creating apps for Apple products is the most efficient starting point, it's is important not to focus solely on one platform without checking in to see how the others are doing. Be flexible and keep an open mind. As the saying goes, the only constant in life is change, so be ahead of the curve and anticipate it as much as you can.

APPLE—IPHONE/IPAD/IPOD

Apple customers are fanatics. They will wait outside an Apple store for hours in the freezing cold to buy their products.

Do you see people standing in line for the products of other platforms? No way. They don't have the same type of loyal and raving fans. You can

Table 1.1
Platforms Available in the App Market

Name	Established	Owner	Available Apps	Download Count	Device Platform
App Store	July 10, 2008	Apple	495,516 (October 2011)	18 billion total (October 2011)	iOS
App World	April 1, 2009	RIM	42,893 (September 2011)	3 million daily (May 2011)	Blackberry OS
Android Market	October 22, 2008	Google	280,360 (September 2011) estimated 550,000 (October 2011)	6 billion total (August 2011)	Android
Windows Phone Marketplace	October 21, 2010	Microsoft	35,600 (October 2011)	12 per person per month (March 2011)	Windows Phone 7

create apps for Android and BlackBerry as well. Almost everything I teach you in this book will rock your apps, regardless of what platform you choose, but I recommend starting with Apple, especially if you're a newbie.

> Alan Johansen is another successful appreneur with zero coding experience. In two years, working as a solo apprenuer, he launched 30 apps, which have been downloaded over 11 million times.
>
> Alan has seen the Apple App Store evolve over the years and believes it is in its infancy. He says, "It's refreshing to see the app stores support and reward independent developers. It's refreshing to see them promote independent titles (instead of only promoting their own titles)."

GOOGLE ANDROID

Android is the second-largest mobile platform on the market and is available on more than 100 devices made by different manufacturers. It's an open-source platform, which allows manufacturers of smartphones to adapt and use it for their devices without any costs. This has made Android the number one mobile operating system in the world.

Even though Apple sells more apps on its iPhones, Android is used on more phones. Year after year, Android has made the biggest gains in these markets, predominantly taking market share away from Apple's iOS and RIM's BlackBerry.

But the research group Kantar Worldpanel Comtech believes that Apple's iOS will make new advances against Android in the United States, as the iPhone is made available to more carriers. Regardless of this, you should consider Android as the second platform you create apps for after making some money on Apple's iOS apps.

BLACKBERRY

The BlackBerry app world is growing, too, at a steady pace of 69 percent per year. However, at this time, BlackBerry's 772 million app downloads is dwarfed compared to Apple's over 18 billion and Android's over 6 billion downloads.

SETTING UP SHOP

The app business has practically zero overhead. I have no office, no equipment, and no employees. I have a Macbook-Pro and an iPhone, and that's it. I run everything from my iPhone, even the daily management of independent contractors. I use my apps to advertise each other, so I have little to no marketing costs.

What other business offers this kind of freedom? Few others, if any, can be run without an office and from anywhere in the world. You might not want to stay in a beach hut in Fiji, see the Seven Wonders of the World, or swim with sharks, but I'm sure you would love to do other things with your extra time.

To start an app business, you need to sign up as a developer with the platform for which you're looking to create apps. Don't be intimidated by the word *developer*. It doesn't mean you have to be the programmer. It's simply the name used for somebody who publishes apps. (We cover outsourcing the programming of your apps in Chapter 5.) All you have to do is set up a "developer account" so you can offer your apps for sale in one of the app stores.

Here are the links for signing up with the different platforms and a brief overview of the requirements for each.

- **Apple iOS** (http://developer.apple.com/programs/register/)—Registration requirements include a fee of $99 per year and accepting the terms of service.
- **Android** (http://developer.android.com/guide/index.html)—Registration requirements include a fee of $25 per year and accepting the terms of service.
- **BlackBerry** (http://us.blackberry.com/developers/)—Registration requirements include a $200 fee for every 10 apps you publish. You must have a BlackBerry World App Vendor Agreement in place with RIM, the creator of BlackBerry to distribute apps.

FUTURE TRENDS

As mentioned earlier, consumers love the convenience of instantly getting something they want. People like the ability to see their loved ones during a phone call. Text messaging is outpacing e-mail and voicemail messages because it's simple and immediate communication. Apps fit in with this on-the-go lifestyle.

As the price of phones drop and more people buy smartphones, the app market will be expanding even faster. People's desire and immediate need for real-time information is spreading like wildfire.

The mobile lifestyle is here to stay. The trends all point to an increasingly mobile lifestyle, which means more opportunity for developers.

TOP 10 APP TRENDS

Looking into the crystal ball of the app industry, research firm Gartner, Inc., predicts these top 10 trends:

1. *Location-based services.* More consumers will use apps that offer more intelligent service based on their current geographic location.
2. *Social networking.* People will spend more time socializing online, using apps that support activities such as web conversations and photo sharing.
3. *Mobile search.* People will integrate information searches with action, such as ordering a pizza or finding a tennis store.
4. *Mobile commerce.* Consumers will buy more products using their phones.
5. *Mobile payment.* Customers at stores will pay for goods and services through their phones.
6. *Context-aware service.* Apps will offer consumers more personalized experiences by customizing services based on personal interests, history, schedule, favorite activities, and more.
7. *Object recognition.* Apps will allow consumers to recognize the user's surroundings, including specific objects of interest. The apps will rely on the camera functions to do this.
8. *Mobile instant messaging.* Mobile instant messaging systems will start to integrate more interactive elements, such as video. Such app services may replace traditional phone use.
9. *Mobile e-mail.* More people will send and receive e-mails via their mobile phones.
10. *Mobile video.* Mobile phones will have bigger screens and higher resolutions. Meanwhile, phone carriers will partner with video services, such as YouTube and Vimeo to offer high-definition viewing through phones.

BUILD A GOLD MINE

The stats show you that the app industry is the next gold rush. However, you have to treat this like a business and not a get-rich-quick scheme. Your gold mine needs to be supported by a solid foundation: a positive and focused mindset and the skills to understand the market and grow your business.

In the next chapter, I share with you the winning mindset for making money in the app business. It will require a shift in thinking and an open mind, but the rewards can be substantial. Your mindset is the key to building a thriving business and the life you want.

What I Learned

1.
2.
3.

Actions to Take

1. Sign up as a developer on the Apple iOS platform.

2

Install This First

The App Millionaire Mindset

I've missed more than 9,000 shots in my career. I've lost almost 300 games. 26 times, I've been trusted to take the game winning shot and missed. I've failed over and over and over again in my life. And that is why I succeed.

—Michael Jordan

After my car accident, I spent over a year and a half in post-op rehabilitation. The doctors told me I wouldn't be able to use my dominant arm in a normal way again.

What?

An avalanche of thoughts crashed through my head.

No more basketball? No throwing a baseball with the kids I don't even have yet? I'm not even married. How is a woman going to feel about being with me now? I can't hold a door open for her anymore. How can I have sex if I can't hold myself up? I can't drive? I can't write? I'm a man. How am I going to have a full life for myself and my family if I can't use my arm? *I'm only 27 years old!!!*

These thoughts screamed in my head, echoing in an endless dark cave. Although I had moments when I was driven and determined to prove the doctors wrong, I was crushed inside and scared.

Each day, I went through two hours of torturous physical therapy, trying to rebuild the muscles in my left arm, straining to develop some sort of range of motion. Sheer pain pulsated throughout my body, turning into total and complete despair after each session. After the daily battle, I would inhale pain medication and sit up in my oversized La-Z-Boy in agony for the remainder of the day, defeated.

I had the same questions before the accident that many people have, like, *What was my life about?* and *What was I going to do next?* Afterwards, I had other questions too: How was I going to regain the use of my arm? If that weren't enough of a problem, how would I make enough money to pay the $100,000 in medical bills I had racked up?

The pain was excruciating, and since I wasn't able to lie down, I couldn't sleep. At one point, I hadn't slept well for five weeks, and the fatigue was taking a mental and physical toll. I was in so much pain, I felt like giving up for good.

That's when I hit my lowest point. I was alone one afternoon, and my mind went to a dark place. I wasn't even grateful for surviving such a horrid wreck. Instead, I wondered why I had survived.

I was awake, heavily medicated, tears streaming down my face.

Suddenly, something inside me screamed, like a loudspeaker at an airport.

You were meant for more than this! the voice said. *Fight, Chad. Fight! Don't give up. You can still have the life you want. You just have to believe and make it happen.*

I'm not sure what happened that day, or where that voice came from. Call it my Creator, call it my voice of reason, but that voice had such a profound effect on me that I knew I had no choice. I had to listen and from that moment on, in all that darkness, I had a glimpse of the possibility of a life that I had all but given up on, and hope began to slide in through the cracks.

Everything started to change. For the first time, I understood the importance and the strength of one's own beliefs and faith. I decided I didn't want to be an extra in the movie of my life anymore. It was time to be the writer and the producer.

I haven't looked back since and guess what? The movie of my life has been an epic that gets better every day.

As you embark on this journey, I ask you to listen to your own loudspeaker. Believe in yourself and your app business. Trust your inner cheerleader, and silence the nagging victim because great things will come of your efforts.

No matter what enterprise you're launching, whether it's apps or apple pies, having a winning mindset is most important. In fact, it's the most critical part of the app business and the reason some people make millions as others fail.

WINNING BELIEFS IN THE APP BUSINESS

Maybe you're thinking, "But Chad, I've got a good mindset. After all, I'm reading this book, right?"

Well, in the app business your mind plays games with you by saying things like, "I don't know software . . . I don't have the money . . . I've never run a business."

We all have beliefs that affect everything we do. When we shift our core beliefs, we shift our outcomes. Let me help you change your beliefs about running an app business, so you can have the life you want.

At the events and parties I go to, I hear people's doubts about this business. I don't blame them. I was there once and had to go through my own journey to get through my limiting beliefs.

Here are some of the most common fears I hear from people:

- *"I've never done this before . . . I don't have the experience . . . I don't have the background."*

  I was in that same spot. But I found successful people to learn from.

  If you want to achieve success, all you need to do is find a way to model those who have succeeded. Find someone to model as soon as possible.

  Start small and learn over time. You may make some mistakes, but you will develop more confidence and knowledge. Before you know it, others will model you.

- *"It's difficult . . . I don't understand it . . . I'm not smart enough."*

  Anyone can do this business, even if you don't understand it. Like anything in life, you have to start somewhere. This is one of the easiest businesses to get into, because the market is telling you what to do. All you have to do is to listen.

  This business is about looking at the market, understanding it, and giving users what you think they want. You may not hit home runs your first time at bat, but you have to keep getting up to swing throughout the whole game.

- *"I'm not a computer person," "I'm not a developer," "I'm not a coder."*

  Neither am I. I don't know how to program anything and don't want to. You can get into the app business regardless of your computer skills. If you can draw an app idea and convey the concept to programmers or designers, then they can do the work for you. Even if you know how to code, I recommend hiring others to do most of it so you can focus more on running and building the business.

  Two of my appreneur friends had software engineering degrees when they started creating apps. They soon realized they had to outsource to other programmers, so they could be appreneurs.

- *"It costs a lot of money . . . I don't have money to waste . . . I don't have money to set up an app business."*

You don't need a lot of money to start. It costs anywhere from $500 to $5,000 to develop simple apps. As soon as you launch your app, depending on your sales, you could see money hit your bank account within two months.

I got started by being in a crazy amount of debt, borrowing money from my stepfather for a Hail Mary shot. I didn't have any employees and outsourced all the work.

In this business, the barrier to entry is ridiculously low. You don't need a degree. You don't have to get a license like a stock-broker. You don't have to invest $60,000 or more for a four-year education. You don't have to pay $50,000 for a franchise license. You don't need many employees, lots of equipment, overhead, or commercial space.

Even if you mess up, the loss is relatively small. If you keep going, and learn from your mistakes, you will have an opportunity to make a lot of money.

- *"I'm not a businessperson . . . I don't know how to be an entrepreneur."*

You don't have to be. And this is much easier to do than most other kinds of businesses.

Apple does the distribution so you can spend your time on marketing. If you can keep testing the market and course correct based on data, you can run a successful app business.

- *"I don't have enough time . . . I've got a full-time job . . . I don't have enough time to learn this."*

This business is about getting your time and life back. Even if you're making $100,000 a year at your full-time job, is it worth it if you never see your kids or spouse or don't have a fulfilling life?

The beauty with this business is that you have the option to start part-time, and as you learn more and gain more confidence, you can take bigger steps.

When you quit your job because you doubled your income, you'll have more time than you know what to do with, and that's what this business gives you. Time and freedom to do what you want, when you want, and with whom you want.

- *"I've lost my confidence . . . I've been down since I lost my job . . . The recession has been hard on me."*

When I was a kid, I used to play football in my neighborhood with a guy called Smalls. We used to pick on him. He was probably 110 pounds soaking wet, but you could hit this guy and he would hardly ever go down. If he did, he would pop right back up as if nothing had happened. It didn't make any sense because everyone was bigger and stronger than he was. How the heck did he take such big hits and remain on his feet? So, one day at the lunchroom in school, I walked up to him:

"Smalls, how do you stay on your feet when you get hit so hard on the football field?" I asked. "You are so small. What's your secret?"
"Do you really wanna know?"
"Yeah, I really wanna know."
"I keep moving," he said.
"What?"
"Watch my feet when I get hit," he said. "I never stop. Yeah, I can take a hit; yeah I can get pushed around, but my feet never stop moving. I don't allow myself to think I'm going to fall, so I don't."

My first reaction was that what he said was pretty stupid, but after thinking about it, I saw the deeper meaning. It made sense. That's how it is in life, in business, and everything else. We all know that you have to get back up if you fall down, but what a lot of us seem to miss is that oftentimes when we think we are falling, we give up, and allow gravity to take over. Most times, we are much closer to staying on our feet than we think. Usually, it's a matter of hanging in there and moving your feet a little longer until, eventually you find yourself running for a touchdown.

Use your current situation as the fuel that empowers you to take action. Use it as leverage. The way I see it is you have two choices. Do nothing and complain, or use your resources to turn your situation around. If my truck had not flipped over four times on the interstate, I'm not sure I would have had the leverage I needed for change. Pain can be our best gift and biggest weapon to succeed as long as we convince ourselves to see it that way.

- *"Only a few people make money in this business. . . . The big players are hard to compete against. . . . It's too hard to make money because every idea is taken."*

The big players are like you. This industry is in its infancy, and anyone can make an app as well as they can. They might have big marketing dollars, but you can still market your app with no to little money as you'll see later on in the book.

What makes the app business unique is that the big players are on the same playing field as everyone else. They have the same questions and challenges as you and I will have.

The industry is just getting started. As I said before, it's like the Internet when e-commerce began. You have the opportunity to grow with the industry. You don't have to come up with new ideas. If you improve on existing app ideas, you can make money.

- *"I'm in for the gold rush. . . . I can make a lot of money without working."*

Many people are joining the app gold rush with a get-rich-quick mentality and unrealistic expectations. Don't let this be you. This book gives you the tools to think like a business owner with a map to find the gold. You have to work, but you won't have to struggle and let life pass you by in the process.

This is not a one-time app lottery, and you can't treat it as such. We all want instant gratification, but if you think of this as a long-term business, it will grow and be a sustainable source of income.

- *"Just because someone else was successful, it doesn't mean I will be."*

That's right. The most important thing in this business is your mindset. We can be our biggest enemy or our greatest hero, but ultimately, we have the freedom to choose and decide what we are going to focus on.

CREATE A GOLDEN MINDSET

You must create beliefs around wealth that allow you to get out of your own way. Learn to see the opportunities instead of all the reasons things won't work or haven't worked in the past. By shifting your beliefs, you can turn challenges into opportunities to learn and grow.

Anthony Robbins changed my life in many ways. While I was recovering in the hospital from my car accident, someone gave me his "Get The Edge" program as a gift. His words unlocked a part of me I didn't know existed.

I realized that up to that point in my life, I had focused on the tools of business. I asked questions like, "How do I get more sales?" "How can I get better at marketing?" "Whom do I hire to work for me?"

Tony Robbins taught me to ask questions on a deeper level: "What kind of life do I want to live?" "What's important to me?" "How do

I want to express myself?" "What do I want from making money?" "What's my mission?" These questions made me think about business and life in a different way, weeding out the junk and giving myself true alignment.

I realized that to live the life I wanted, I needed to do a major shift of my mindset and realign my core beliefs.

When I changed my beliefs, I started to have a tenacious mindset. I knew what I wanted, I wasn't going to let other people's agendas get in my way, and I was happy. I realized that without my body, without my inner clarity and peace, I was nothing. That gave me a sense of gratitude. I had a different energy and a strong, positive mind. That made my business and way of life exciting every day.

Look, you don't have to go through a major traumatic event the way I did to learn these lessons, and I would never wish what happened to me on anyone. Do whatever you need to strengthen your mental and emotional muscles. My accident radically changed me because I felt I was given a second chance, and I wasn't going to abuse that gift. Your second chance and new beginning starts now.

QUALITIES OF A WINNING MINDSET

The following are key elements of a winning mindset, along with actions you can take to thrive in the app world and in your life.

Know Your "Why"

Ask yourself, "Why do I want to make money in the app business?" Everyone needs a driving force, so hone in on yours, and you've won half the battle for success. This *why* might be unique to you, or similar to the "why" of other appreneurs.

Whatever it is, you cannot be successful without knowing your primary reason for success. It could be that you want to travel around the world, pay for your child's college tuition, do charity work, support your aging parents, or help the environment.

Show me people with a big enough reason *why* they want to accomplish something, and I can assure you, it's only a matter of time before it becomes a reality. What's your "why?"

Powerful Questions

As you can see from the previous section, asking thoughtful questions is more important than having quick answers.

Powerful questions trigger your brain to search for powerful answers. I've learned that high levels of enlightenment and incredible success are a direct result of the quality of the questions you ask yourself on a consistent basis.

Be sure to ask yourself powerful questions every day. The results will amaze you. What will manifest from this habit will propel your business to new levels.

Here are some powerful questions you can ask yourself before launching your app business:

- What will I do with the newfound freedom that I'll have?
- Who am I doing this for? Why?
- How will being successful at this change the lives of my loved ones?
- What am I committed to doing to guarantee my success?

Another powerful tool is taking immediate action however small the step may seem. Humor me, grab a piece of paper, and take five minutes to consider and answer these questions.

In later chapters, I share with you more detailed questions you can ask, related directly to specific parts of your business.

Vision/Outcomes

Create a vision that ignites your passion. Then specify outcomes you want from that vision.

Creating a vision for your business is essential for figuring out where you want to go. Would you jump into a car and drive without knowing your destination? Well, we know that many people go through life's motions half-asleep, taking on task after task to keep themselves in busy mode. I'm assuming if you picked up a book about creating a successful app business and reinventing your life, that isn't your style.

When you create a vision, continue your inner dialogue until you get a better understanding of your motivation:

You might say, "I want to make a certain amount of money."

Okay, well why do you really want this?

You might say, "I want to pay off debt, and not worry about money all the time."

Okay, well, what will that give you?

Maybe "It will lift a heavy burden off my shoulders and allow me to feel free."

Well, why is this freedom so important?

"It will allow me to feel good again. I will be able to spend time with my family, see them laugh, have fun, and enjoy life. I can catch up with old friends, travel to places I've always wanted to see, experience life in new ways, remember what it felt like to be a kid again, revive the dreams that I let die, etc."

Keep delving deeper because the initial responses are usually super-ficial and don't reveal the real motivations behind our actions. Usually when you do this, at some point something inside of you will click. You will feel like you are ready to explode, fully alive, and passionate. That's when you will have reached your true vision. When you are challenged to be specific about your goals, the truth comes out, and you will manifest what you want.

Once you have that clarity, set your outcomes or goals around that to accomplish the vision.

For another example, ask yourself, "What is the vision for my company, and what do I want to create?"

Be specific. Make it emotional, something you would strive for, and create your compelling future now. Relate your outcome to something tangible.

For instance, "If I can make $10,000 a month, I'm going to travel to Italy and paddle around in a boat through the Grand Canal of Venice." Maybe it's a yearly goal with a reward, like, "I'll fully fund my kids' education," "I'll buy a bigger house," or "I'll get myself out of debt."

Write it where you will see it throughout your day. It will keep you motivated and give you the energy to overcome unforeseen and uncon-trollable obstacles that could sidetrack you from the life that you know you deserve.

I write my outcomes on the bathroom mirror, using an erasable black marker because I know that every morning, I'll go to the bathroom, brush my teeth, and look in the mirror.

Over the years, I've written things like, "Get to $1,000/month cash flow," "Travel somewhere exotic," or "Sell my app business for seven figures."

Seeing those every day made them happen faster, and instantly gave me the motivation I needed to push through that day's challenges.

Faith/Optimism

Whatever your goal, you must consistently believe you have a way to achieve it, and you must be resolute in this belief. To attract success, learn to see it, feel it, and manifest it.

I've always had faith on a superficial level but never truly allowed myself to embrace it. After my accident and hearing the voice that pulled my mind out of that dark place, I can't deny the power of something greater than myself. I realize that not everyone has an experience like this, but I urge you to connect or reconnect to whatever higher power you believe in. It will be a game changer for you.

Passion

You need to be enthusiastic about your business and whatever you do in life. Since you're spending time building this new enterprise, you are in a position to make it feel less like work and more like fun and play, otherwise you will burn out quickly.

This happens to everyone at one job or another, and your goal is to set this up so it doesn't feel like a job. It should be fulfilling and feel more like something you get to do, not something you have to do. Once you create this vision, the momentum will pull you forward effortlessly, like a ski lift pulling you straight up a mountain of cash.

To accomplish this, focus on creating apps you can enjoy and make money with. For example, if you like playing video games, you probably have an interest and knowledge in that category of apps. If you're a photography buff, and you see that photography apps are popular, you can spend some time in that category and come up with something that other photography buffs like yourself will enjoy.

Attitude

When I was in the hospital, a buddy sent me a quote from Stephen Covey, author of *Seven Habits of Highly Effective People*. It was profound enough to help me change my attitude, and transform my thinking.

It talks about another percentage, called the 90/10 Principle. It says this: "Ten percent of life is made up of what happens to you. Ninety percent of life is decided by how you react."

What does this mean? We have little control over what actually happens to us in life. We cannot stop a car from breaking down, a plane from arriving late, the driver who cuts us off in traffic, or a deer that jumps in front of our truck. But we have almost complete control over how we interpret and react to the events of life.

We cannot control a red light, but we can control whether we get mad or shrug it off while continuing to jam out to the radio. Simple, yet profoundly effective.

After I learned the 90/10 Principle, I realized that life isn't meant to be so hard. Maybe I was sabotaging myself with my negative attitude and making things worse for myself. I had a choice of what to focus on, and what meaning I was going to give the events of my life.

I realized that whenever people asked about my real estate business, I would say, "Oh, it's horrible. It's so hard. I'm not making any money." I felt weak, and people around me would feel miserable, too. It became an endless cycle of negativity that manifested bad results and bad feelings.

When I shifted my attitude, I developed an attitude of optimism and confidence. That made a huge difference, and took me on a new course, with a new destination.

In the app business, things are always changing. You never know what's going to happen. You will be challenged, but if you train yourself to have a strong, positive mind. You will have a competitive advantage over 99 percent of other developers/appreneurs.

Plan

Yes, saying you should plan is obvious, but it is true, and I've only realized the importance of this in the last few years. If you don't plan thoroughly, then you are planning to fail miserably. In business, you'll get much better results if you plan effectively, instead of sprinting in like a testosterone-fueled bull running the streets of Pamplona, Spain.

Your plan doesn't need to be so complicated that it prevents you from taking any action. Being present and aware versus uncertain about your business is more profitable and gives you the certainty and clarity you need to forge ahead.

Flexibility

Change is constant in this business or any business for that matter. As a business owner, you must be open to radically changing your apps and strategies that aren't serving you, and cut the fat immediately.

The first version of any app rarely succeeds. The goal is to remain objective and adapt as soon as you have real data that give you clarity in a particular area. If you don't stay flexible, you will waste time and money and will lose motivation. If you constantly refine, you have a greater chance of succeeding.

Because an idea doesn't work at first, it doesn't mean it won't in the future. A little tweaking or a little time is often all that is needed.

I have had several business failures and not every app brought in the profit I desired, but I learned valuable lessons and then adapted. As long as you track what you're doing, and correct your course, you will keep moving in the right direction.

Leverage/Outsource

I have always been a creator, which means I always have wanted to do more, no matter what I have had on my plate. The problem with that mindset is that I was always working harder and burning myself out without feeling satisfied.

App developers are notorious for this over-indulgence as well.

If you want your business to grow, you need to outsource. You must be able to count on others and let go. Keith Cunningham, an accomplished entrepreneur and speaker, once said, "Growth and control work inversely." The more you want to grow, the more you need to give up control.

Bogged down with billing? Outsource it. Tired of answering e-mail? Outsource it. Can't stand checking on developers? Let someone else do it. Outsource everything that drains your time and motivation. Outsource anything that takes away your ability to grow bigger than yourself, and have fun doing the things you like to do. This will ensure you have gas in the tank for any adventure that comes your way.

Build a great team that supports and enhances what you are doing. This way, you can focus on what you do best, which is visualizing and planning the business.

Presence/Focus

You should treat your business the way you would a new relationship. Become intimate with your business and find the passion. The more you listen to it, nurture it, pay attention to it, and give it value, the stronger your relationship will become. If you don't, you'll be sleeping on the couch in no time, and it's going to be uncomfortable.

When you are present with your business, you will see better results. If you are not present, and if you take it for granted, your business can get off track or you can lose your business altogether.

The Apple App Store is a global economy that's changing every day. If you're not present with your business, constantly adapting and improving, you will get left behind.

It takes discipline to keep your eyes on the prize. You must understand each component of your app business, which analytics can help you do. I recommend you evaluate what's going on in each area of your business: daily, weekly, and monthly. Monitor the market daily, track your results, and make course corrections.

At one point, I was traveling so much that I wasn't working on my business. It's easy to do in this business because you're making money without doing anything, and sometimes you forget. One day while traveling in Canada, I realized my complacency had caught up to me and I needed to shift gears because the numbers were dropping.

I put attention on my business for two to three hours a day for three weeks, but it was focused time. I got present and took the pulse of each section of my company. I knew if our marketing was hitting the mark, and I knew what we needed to change to make customers happy. I made my tweaks and gave my business the fuel it needed. By doing that, income went up 68 percent!

It's not just about "How much money can I make right now?" It's about being present with each step of the process, for the long haul.

Synergy: 1+1 = 1,000,000

Find other like-minded people to help you grow.

One excellent way is through mastermind groups. This is when you join a small group where everyone is focused on giving each other encouragement and practical strategies to succeed. You can share resources and grow together.

Another way is to network with other appreneurs or developers. Find them online, at conferences, and in meet-up groups.

When you network, you will find successful people to model. Surround yourself with people who have a positive mindset and can help you grow. Learn the easy way through their experiences as opposed to having to fall on your face to learn the hard way on your own.

By networking with other appreneurs, I have learned tips that doubled and tripled my income and strengthened my winning mindset. I learn and pick up new ideas from others, and I contribute to their app world as well, growing their business.

As an end note, applying the same techniques in this chapter has given me the mental and physical strength that I needed to overcome my accident and build a successful app company. I have total certainty they will serve you as well.

What I Learned

1.
2.
3.

Actions to Take

1. As yourself these questions and write down the answers:
   o What's my *why*, and how will my life change when I get it?
   o What can I see myself doing in the app business to make money? What's my passion?
   o What do I want to do with the freedom I will have?

o How committed am I to making this work, and how important is it that I succeed?

o When and how am I going to check in daily on my winning mindset?

o Who else is going to benefit from this new way of life and money, and what will that mean to them and to me?

2. Write down the new empowering beliefs that you're going to associate with every day.

Discover the New World

The App Store

The real voyage of discovery consists not in seeking new landscapes but in having new eyes.

—Marcel Proust

"Happy Friday," the bank teller said.

"Thank you. This is one of the best days of my life!" I said, smiling from ear to ear.

Cashing the $73,322 check gave me one of the best feelings I had ever experienced. I was ecstatic because it was more money than I had made throughout my entire life, and it was in one real estate deal.

That deal meant more than just money to me. It symbolized victory and a new life with new opportunities. I had worked my butt off, struggled, through blood, sweat, and tears to realize the American Dream that I grew up fantasizing about.

While most guys in their early twenties were partying, chasing girls, or vegging out and doing nothing, I found myself reading books, studying local real estate markets, learning from successful real estate investors, and of course chasing girls. I was hoping to emulate them and live the life they were living. Holding the check that day after the closing, I was grateful. All the hard work had paid off, and I had made it.

On January 6, 2006, at the age of 24, I moved back to Myrtle Beach, South Carolina, where I had gone to college, to start a real estate company, thinking I had this industry on lockdown.

Everyone was making money in real estate, and hardly anyone anticipated that the party would end. Less than a year later, without warning, the market tanked, and everything I had planned and worked for fell apart.

When it crashed, all my efforts turned into a pile of bills minus the money to pay them. I burned through the money I had made on my first real estate deal in seven months and had no money left to weather the downturn.

Desperate, I looked to one of my mentors who lived in New York. I was positive he would have the answer, and I became furious when his magic pill was this: "Do whatever you were doing while you were succeeding because I think you have forgotten what you worked so hard to learn."

What the hell was that supposed to mean? I thought. Two weeks later, I was brushing my teeth, and all of a sudden, like someone coming out of a coma, I had my "aha" moment.

I realized I had been looking at the market through the lens of a real estate business owner instead of through the eyes of a customer. I had found success earlier because I became obsessed with researching the market and thinking like customers, meaning the homebuyers. My ability to understand the market had always given me a competitive edge.

I realized that even in a down market, Myrtle Beach was a transient place, and people were still looking for places to live in. I had to figure out where, what kind of homes, and how to find those buyers.

I remembered that when I bought my house, I wanted to be in the best area, with good schools and near the beach. I figured that other people must have specific needs as well, and there must be data that would tell me which areas had the highest number of transactions. So, I researched and found the hottest, most desirable subdivisions that were doing well compared to the rest and decided to park myself there.

My mentor had been right. *If these are the hottest properties*, I then asked myself, *Who's selling houses there, and how are they doing it? What are they doing to attract buyers and/or sellers?*

It turned out that the top real estate agents in those areas were finding buyers through small newspaper ads, and were using specific language. That was it. I emulated their marketing strategies and found buyers. I was able to cash in on those buyers and keep my business alive. When the market changed, I trained myself to be present and listen, so I could change strategies and go with it versus fighting it.

The real estate downturn lasted longer than I anticipated, stretching my finances thin, and though it was hard, it was a valuable experience I am grateful for. It was the battlefield where I developed skills I needed to survive in business. I use the same strategies with my app business with fewer headaches. I look at the big picture, research the market, think like a consumer, and emulate the most successful players.

The good news is that you can avoid the battle scars and use these strategies from day one. Listen to the market, and follow the trends. As an appreneur, the more you understand customers and give them what they want, the bigger and more consistent your reward will be.

In this chapter, I take you on a tour of the App Store, so you can navigate this powerful resource like a pro. You'll learn how to spot which criteria people are using when buying apps, and turn the App Store into your own personal ATM.

GATHERING INTELLIGENCE

As with any business, your success will be directly related to your understanding of the marketplace. The App Store is the marketplace of the app business so to understand the market we have to study the App Store. This seems rather obvious, but you won't believe how many developers I meet that don't understand this concept. They don't watch the market, follow the most successful apps, or figure out why those apps are successful.

Most of my success comes from my knowledge of the market. It's as easy as that. I make it a point to check the App Store every day. It's a daily process to see which apps are working and which ones are not. This means downloading them, playing around with them, and seeing how they are marketed.

The more time you spend with apps, the better you'll understand the common traits of successful apps and what users are looking for. The more you think like the customer, the greater your success will be. You need to become an app addict if you want to be a successful supplier. This mindset has been the lifeblood of my success.

For instance, a little while ago, I looked at the top grossing apps, and I noticed a big change. Until recently, many of the top grossing apps were paid apps, but a lot of them have become free (see Figure 3.1). When I noticed this trend, I asked myself what was happening and why. I took a closer look at the top-grossing free apps. I downloaded several of them and saw that developers were beginning to take advantage of in-app purchases by offering lots of additional, useful paid features within the free apps. Apple had introduced in-app purchases as a tool for developers to sell content within their apps some time before that, but it took a while for developers and users to take full advantage of them. Users love that the apps are free, and they can pay for additional features if they want them.

Based on this info, I knew where the action was going and that I had to adapt my business model. I called my developer and started to update my apps so I could increase revenue through in-app purchases. This has been a huge shift in the market, and without monitoring the market daily, I would not have picked up on it.

FIGURE 3.1   Top grossing apps: 19 out of 25 are free.

I see other top developers watching and adjusting to the market constantly as well. The more present and informed you are on what's happening in the marketplace, the quicker you can adjust and capitalize on changing conditions.

READ BETWEEN THE APPS

So, how do you keep pace with the market? The best way to do that is to check out Apple's cheat sheet and study it constantly. The App Store displays the top paid, the top free, and the top-grossing apps (the apps that make the most money including free apps), almost in real time (see Figure 3.2). Apple provides the same lists in the individual app categories.

FIGURE 3.2   Top 25 paid, free, and grossing apps.

This info is golden because it tells us volumes about the market. The best part is this information is accessible at any moment unlike the market info of any other industry.

Review these charts frequently, and look for trends you can take advantage of. That's what I do. This educates me about different pricing models and how successful apps are being designed and marketed. When looking at the market, these are some of the questions to ask:

- Why is this app successful?
- What is its rank and has it been consistent?
- Why do people want this app? (Look at the reviews.)
- Has this app made the customer a raving fan?
- Does this app meet any of my needs?
- Did I become a raving fan after trying it?
- Does this app provoke an impulse buy?
- Will the customer use it again?
- How are developers marketing to their customers? (Check out the screen shots, icon design, and descriptions.)
- What else can I learn from the company that created the app?
- What is the competitive advantage of this app?

Be curious, and constantly ask lots of questions. This will help you uncover clues to success. This research is simple, costs nothing, and is lots of fun. You will be downloading and playing games and testing other apps as well. Rediscover your inner child and have fun.

It's important to write down what you observe so you can use that information to your advantage. Instead of saying, "I think this is what's going to work," or "My buddy told me this app is great so I'm going for it," let objective data lead you. Few apps, if any, become successful by chance. After you do this for some time, you will develop an uncanny sixth sense for what works in the market and what doesn't.

Every second you spend with an app is part of your market research, which will make you more savvy and knowledgeable as an appreneur. Even as your business grows, keep learning about new apps. You can discover new ideas and different device capabilities.

When should you research the market? Utilize your idle time as much as possible. Checking the pulse of the App Store takes 5 to 10 minutes. In addition to that, schedule time to focus on your market research when in front of a computer. This will give you the ability to see more on the screen and more easily note any trends.

TWO TYPES OF APPS

Though you will find many categories of apps in the App Store, such as Games, Entertainment, Utility, and Productivity, only two types of apps exist: those designed for entertainment purposes and those designed for productivity. I am not referring to the entertainment and utility categories in the App Store. Instead, I divide apps into two groups because that simplifies the process of researching and understanding the demographics of app users.

Entertainment apps can range from action games, puzzles, and fake IQ tests, to gun simulators, prank apps, and many others. They offer fun, are mindless, and are usually used to pass the time as a wanted distraction. They usually require little effort or thought from the user.

The top-grossing entertainment apps aren't just action games like Angry Birds. They can be apps, like Talking Ben, in which an animated interactive dog repeats all of your words in a funny lower pitched voice. Another example is an app called Top Girl, which simulates a virtual world, that lets a girl walk around, get a boyfriend, buy clothes for him, and more. This isn't my cup of tea, but enough people love it and keep it highly ranked.

Another entertainment app that always seems to be one of the top five in the list of highest grossing apps is Tap Pet Hotel. Inside is a virtual world where the user has to care for a pet on a daily basis, paying to upgrade to feed or to teach the pet a new trick. This virtual world uses fake currency as its system of rewards, which hooks customers and makes them raving fans.

The ingenuity of the app lies in its deeper goal: hooking the user into returning.

I would never have guessed in a million years that a virtual pet hotel app would be as popular as it is. I would never have come up with it myself. This is a good example of remaining objective when judging whether an app could work. Keep emotions and personal preferences out of your decision making. I don't care how much success I have, or what I think I may know, I always let the data lead me.

As of this writing, people put the biggest premium on being entertained and letting loose with games. Seventy-five of the top 100 paid applications are entertainment apps.

Only 10 percent of the top 100 highest grossing apps are utility based. I think this uneven demand will remain for a while because of the entertainment focus of the iPhone user.

On the other hand, utility apps make the world more convenient, helping people with everyday tasks. Examples include apps that turn your iPhone into a flashlight, track diets, create grocery lists, perform currency conversions, or send voice memos as text messages. These apps significantly extend the functionality and usefulness of smartphones. Ever visit a new city, and have no idea of what to do, or where to get a decent meal? Well, within seconds, an app like Yelp can help.

Utility-based apps are becoming more prevalent as more established businesses are creating apps to meet the mobile lifestyle demands of their customers. These apps are designed to support a company's existing business and they are acting as tools for brand recognition. More companies are catapulting themselves into the mobile arena in hopes of gaining visibility and awareness. Apps are becoming the new website, and businessowners are recognizing the value and adapting quickly. This is why utility apps will continue to increase.

APP DISCOVERY

Another important nugget when it comes to making money in the app business is how easily customers discover apps. Without users finding your products, no sale can occur. Customers have two ways to find an app: through a keyword search on the App Store or through browsing its top charts. This means an app's visibility is determined by the app's search and top chart rankings. Therefore, you must do whatever you can to monitor and improve your rankings at all times. Most developers don't monitor their rankings consistently because they think they don't have any control over them. This couldn't be further from the truth. These rankings are so important that I use them daily to make crucial decisions about my apps.

Until recently app rankings were based on the number of downloads each app was receiving. Then Apple slightly modified its ranking algorithm to include other variables such as frequency and duration of app usage. After this change, frequently used apps like the Facebook app moved up in the charts.

The App Store analyzer, Chomp, publishes a series of metrics relating to both the App Store (Apple) and Android Market (Google) each month, which provides valuable insight into the mobile market (see Figure 3.3). Take note of these statistics, especially the interests and spending habits of consumers.

The illustration below shows that 83 percent of all searches on the App Store are based on functionality or a category, such as puzzle games or photography, rather than a specific name of an application. With more than 500,000 applications on the App Store, users probably know few, if any, apps by name. This type of insight can mean the difference between

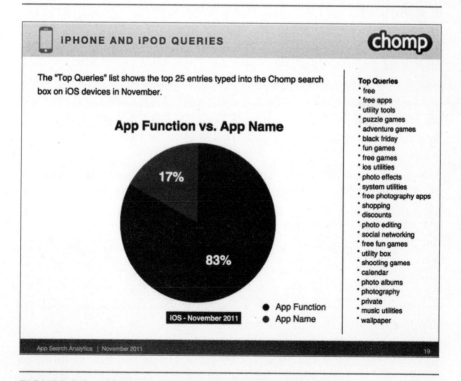

FIGURE 3.3   Chomp's iOS Search Analytics Report.

sleeping on your buddy's futon or living in a penthouse overlooking San Francisco Bay.

HOW DEVELOPERS MAKE MONEY

You won't have to be a cheesy used car salesman or wear a suit and tie to sell apps. This can be the easy part when it comes to your business. Apple has single-handedly revolutionized the world of software distribution. Once you create an app and publish it on the App Store, it becomes accessible on every iOS device in over 120 countries. (See Figure 3.4.)

The nice thing for developers is that these little 99-cent transactions can snowball into millions of dollars, especially when they happen around the world at all hours of the day.

Paid apps can cost anywhere from 99 cents to $999 per download. Most paid apps are 99 cents like the highly successful apps Doodle Jump or AppZilla, but a small number of apps like the bar exam prep app called BarMax or the exclusive VIP venues app called iVip Black go for as high as $999.

With such a large range, you might be asking yourself what's the best price point for an app. Those dollar stores you see all over the place have it figured out. Like discount stores that offer everything on their shelves for under a dollar, the sweet spot for paid app pricing is 99 cents.

This is the most lucrative price point for developers and I don't recommend selling apps at higher prices because the market share is too small. You might make money, but you are less likely to make big bucks, and it's risky.

Becoming a millionaire by selling millions of downloads at 99 cents is easier than 50,000 downloads for $20 each. The lower price gives you an easier sell, and the App Store top charts ranking you get from having more downloads gives you more visibility.

My goal is to help you create the lifestyle you want sooner than later, which means making as much money as possible and as quickly as possible. If you go the route of the 99-cent app, or even the free app model, you are more likely to have the market share and funds to support the lifestyle that you want.

Some high-end game companies, like Electronic Arts, charge more for its paid apps, such as $4.99 versus 99 cents. Unless you have millions of dollars in brand recognition, higher price points are not the way to go.

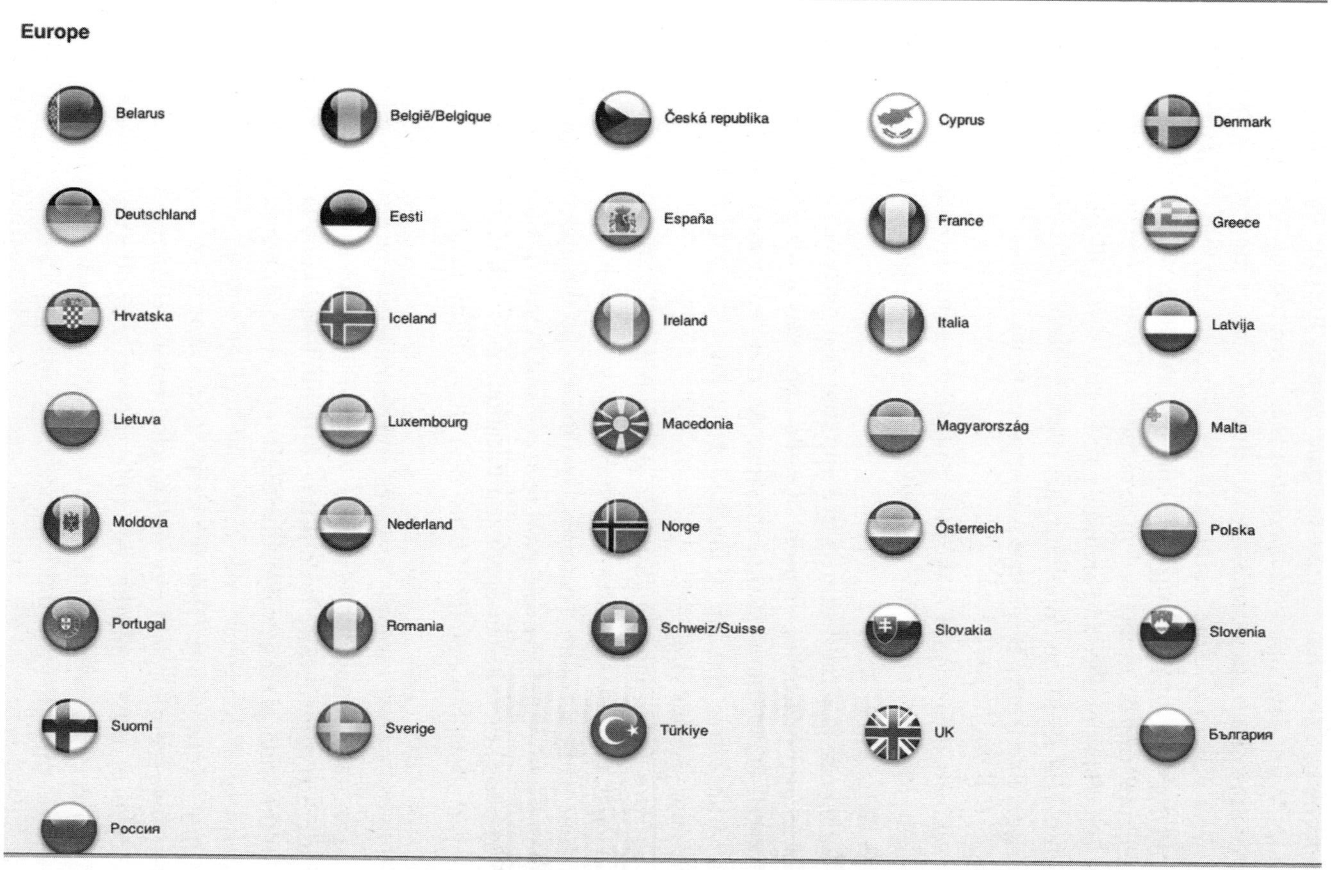

Europe

FIGURE 3.4   App stores in Europe.

45

Even though paid apps continue to be a major source of revenue for developers, free apps have surpassed paid apps as the primary source of revenue. Many developers have created their own money tree by offering free apps. Free apps can make developers a lot of money, and they are a great way to give the market a litmus test. You can find out if users have an appetite for your app and adjust your strategy accordingly.

Free apps can be monetized in a number of ways. Sometimes, they have basic functionality and are used to advertise their full-featured paid versions. This tool is so important that even the developers of successful paid apps, like Angry Birds, use free apps to funnel traffic to their paid apps.

Developers occasionally make their paid apps free for a limited amount of time to increase their app's user base more quickly and give the app a chance to go viral.

Another use is a full-featured free app that is monetized by advertising or in-app purchases. If users like the app, they'll continue to buy additional paid features within the app. As you can imagine, multiple sales within a free app can be much more lucrative for a developer then a one-time upfront sale.

Free apps fail when the customer gets bored and stops using them. An inactive customer is a lost customer, which means less money going into your bank account. Therefore, you must keep the user engaged by providing additional free and paid features and benefits. Allowing users to brag about their achievements on Facebook or other platforms gives an app a shot at going viral. This type of visibility gets more people interested in the app.

Songify is a great example of a free app that uses the techniques mentioned above. The app allows users to create songs using their own voice. The user's recorded voice is auto-tuned (think T-Pain) and layered over one of the soundtracks provided with the app. The result is a surprising masterpiece of fun music that turns the average shower singer into a Grammy award winner. This app keeps users engaged because they can create new recordings and mix and match them with different songs. The developers monetize and add more value to Songify by offering additional songs users can purchase for 99 cents. Users can post their creations and show them off to the world using Facebook, email, or Twitter.

We will go over app revenue models in much greater detail in Chapter 9, but for now, you must be aware of the power of free app monetization and ensure you have included free apps in your research.

THE IMPULSE BUY

Apps appeal to buyers for many reasons. One main reason so much money is spent on them, and why a recession is unlikely to adversely affect the core business model is because app sales are instantaneous micro-transactions. It's easy to act on impulse if instant gratification is only 99 cents and a five-second download away.

In the consumer's mind, spending 99 cents is not a big deal and doesn't require much contemplation, especially when people have purchased a relatively expensive device like a smartphone. In his blog, rocksaucestudios .com, John Gholson nicely paraphrases this behavior: "Ninety-nine cents is the perfect price for an impulse buy, and it rarely feels like a loss because a little digging in your couch cushions or car console means another dollar is right around the corner."

The impulse buy happens in the blink of an eye, with a specific purchase process. I tested this with many users and found that, in the App Store, the average customer goes through the same six-step process when buying an app. Check out the following screen capture of the popular game, Flight Control, as you follow along:

1. They discover the app by searching or browsing the App Store (see Figures 3.5 and 3.6).
2. They check out the app's icon. People are visual. They like interesting icons that tell them what the app does, like a camera for a photo app. Flight Control's icon has a big plane on it and the cartoon vibe tips users off that it's a game.
3. Next, the customers read the title and glance at the rating; Flight Control. The title says it all. "If you want something exciting, this is your game." With 9,060 ratings and 4.5 stars, there's no question about the app's popularity.
4. The customers' eyes then fall on the description, which they scan as they move down to the screen shots. (See Figure 3.7.)

FIGURE 3.5 Discovered through search.

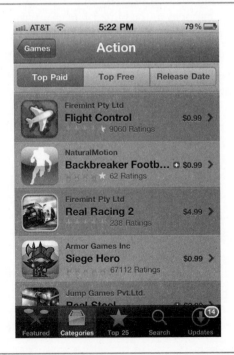

FIGURE 3.6 Discovered through browsing.

FIGURE 3.7   Icon, name, ratings, and description.

5. The screen shots provide great pictures and banner instructions serving as a visual app description. (See Figure 3.8.) Notice a pattern here?

6. Usually they've bought the game after step five. If not, they may read a few reviews to ensure other customers liked it. At this point, they're thinking, "Not bad. I guess I will buy it. Everyone else did. And, heck, it's only a dollar." (See Figure 3.9.)

Potential customers go through each part of this process mostly subconsciously, and each step has to funnel users to the next step, or they won't download the app. This process takes about 10 seconds.

FIGURE 3.8 Screenshots with banners.

HOOKING THE CUSTOMER

So, how do you to turn the impulse buyer into a long-term customer? It's well-known in the business world that it is five to seven times harder to get a new customer than it is to keep one. This is no different in the App Store. My tests concluded that you have to show consumers value within 30 seconds, or they will most likely exit your app and delete it forever. If they initially use the app longer than 30 seconds, it's much more likely that you will keep them as customers. As you can imagine, a long-term customer is worth much more then 99 cents because he will buy more

FIGURE 3.9   Reviews.

of your apps, or purchase additional functionality within your apps, or even just click on your banner ads.

I call the 10-second impulse buy together with the 30 seconds to become a customer the 10/30 rule. It's incredibly important and I design all of my apps based on this concept.

TRAITS OF SUCCESSFUL APPS

Every success story differs, but the most successful apps share quite a few common traits. The following list gives you an idea of most of those traits. In the next chapter, I talk about how to use this list when you are brainstorming for app ideas.

When looking at an app, ask yourself if the app has these qualities:

- **Fun/Entertaining**—How much entertainment value does the app provide? Does it bring joy and excitement to users? Does it make them laugh? Like a great movie, a great app keeps users glued to their screens.
- **Intuitive**—The best apps are simple and easy to use. People can figure them out intuitively and quickly. Consumers shouldn't have to read extensive instructions to get started. Angry Birds and Doodle Jump are masters at this.
- **Engaging**—How engaging is the app? Apps should be as engaging as possible while also showing off the innovative capabilities of the device.
- **Addictive**—You can't put it down. You can't wait to get back to it. You're hooked. That's how the best apps win their users.
- **Value**—The app needs to give far more value in people's minds than what they paid. It should be something they use consistently and feel that they benefit from.
- **Cross-cultural**—It's important that apps appeal to the greatest audience possible. The more people who understand and use the app, the greater the likelihood of the app becoming a hit.
- **Great graphics and sounds**—The top apps are like eye candy. They've got great graphics that are a treat to look at. They also incorporate high-quality sounds.
- **Viral**—Word-of-mouth is a huge form of advertisement. When people get really excited about an app, they share it with lots of people. Why not try to take advantage of free marketing?

Below are some of the top paid apps that have stayed successful from day one. They share a lot of the common traits of winning apps mentioned above.

Doodle Jump

Doodle Jump has a cute little green creature that moves towards the top of the screen by jumping on ledges. (See Figure 3.10.) You control him by tilting your phone to the left or right. If you miss one of the ledges, the creature falls down and dies. It's a fun addictive game that amuses the likes of many.

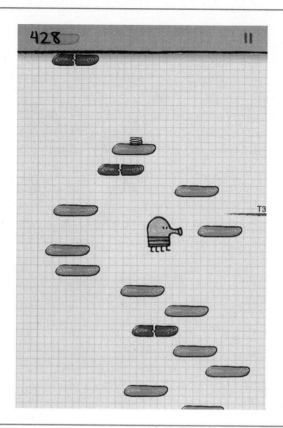

FIGURE 3.10   Doodle Jump.

The Doodle Jump app is a perfect example of a very simple, user-friendly, unique game that anybody can play. That's why it's been so successful. It's so easy that you could give your phone to anyone and they could figure it out immediately. One of the biggest mistakes most developers make is adding too much complexity to their apps making them confusing. Simplicity and ease of use is a common trait among almost all successful apps, and you must take note of this.

Fruit Ninja

Fruit Ninja is a game in which different types of fruit fly up into your screen at an increasing pace. (See Figure 3.11.) The goal is to slice and dice the fruit in half by sliding your finger across the screen at the correct

FIGURE 3.11 Fruit Ninja.

place, using it like a ninja sword. With each piece of fruit you slice, you earn points. Bombs come up as well, so if you get too crazy swiping your finger, you hit a bomb and blow up. Game over.

A lot of highly successful apps such as Fruit Ninja, find ways of incorporating the iPhones innovations like its touch interface in a creative and fun way. This keeps the user engaged, and excited to keep playing.

SERIOUS FUN

When I first looked at the App Store, I was blown away when I saw that the number-one application wasn't about saving the world or revolutionizing the way we conduct business. It was the "Moron Test."

Coming from a serious, traditional real estate background, I was suspicious about the wacky nature of the app market. But then it hit me: most iPhone users are looking for fun, not just productivity.

Because of this, I launched Fingerprint Security Pro when the App Store was still young, and I targeted a younger demographic. My idea was that they could prank their parents and friends—to get them thinking that the iPhone and iPod Touch really did double-up as a fingerprint scanner. One of the reasons it became viral was because of its re-use value; they all showed their friends, who bought it and showed their friends. It was also priced correctly—99 cents. At its peak, Fingerprint Security Pro was listed in the Top 27 overall paid apps. My company's name was Empire Apps and Fingerprint Security became the cornerstone of my App Empire.

The information in this chapter will put you on the fast track to building your own App Empire. In the next chapter, you will learn how to pick winning app ideas.

What I Learned

1.
2.
3.

Actions to Take

1. Look at the range of apps in the App Store to see what the market is offering.
2. Ask people what their favorite apps are and why.
3. Look at successful apps and find out why they are hits, and how you can emulate them.
4. Download at least 20 top apps to understand what appeals to customers.

Your Golden App-ortunity

How to Create Hit Apps

More gold has been mined from the thoughts of men than has been taken from the earth.

—Napoleon Hill

Every New Year's Eve, besides partying like it's the end of the world and drinking alcohol like it's the only beverage left on Earth, my buddy Greg puts together a list of goals he wants to achieve.

Without fail, the number one item on his list is to work out and create that beach body he's been thinking about since he lost it freshman year of college. He becomes consumed with thoughts of how he will start a new fitness regimen January 1, and what his new look will mean to his life, like this is the year it will all change for him.

Year after year, like a broken record, we watch as Greg runs to the local gym without a good thought-out plan and thinking that action alone will yield the results he wants. Although he makes some progress, getting toned up for one or two months, his efforts are unsustainable. He gets hurt or loses interest, and gives up with pure disgust in himself. His New Year's goal becomes shattered again, and he lives the rest of the year telling himself, *This isn't for me*, and *I'm not that guy*, missing out on the outcome he was an inch away from achieving.

Do you know anyone like this?

The same thing happens to most newbie appreneurs. They rush into this business, with lots of hope and dollar signs flashing in front of their eyes, but they don't realize there is a system for everything. Whether you are forging steel abs or creating a million-dollar app biz, you need to learn to funnel your enthusiasm into a system. Otherwise, you will likely give up at the first signs of difficulty. Many appreneurs quit after their first app fails, when they may have been on the verge of succeeding.

It doesn't have to be that way for you. This chapter will be your personal trainer to keep you on track and show you strategies to help you generate successful app ideas. You will learn how to create and implement money-making ideas consistently, analyzing and sifting through each idea you have.

Will all of your ideas be a hit or make money? No, most likely not. However, I can assure you that if you use this process, you won't have to wrestle a leprechaun for that pot of gold at the end of the rainbow.

DON'T FALL IN LOVE WITH YOUR IDEA

I'm sure you've heard the expression: "If you build it, they will come." Most developers believe this is true for apps, but that's not how it works in the app world.

They build an app and expect someone, or a whole lot of someones, to find it immediately and download it. That rarely happens. You have to figure out what people are interested in and the kinds of apps they're downloading, and you build your app based on that insight.

As I explained in Chapter 3, your market research will give you these insights. Make time for market analysis every day. This will help you generate the most lucrative ideas. You will see how consumers are behaving, and it's your job to recognize, understand, track, and take advantage of this insider information.

If you are passionate about a specific subject, that's a good starting point to explore app ideas. It's always advantageous to work on something that you enjoy because you will have more insight on the topic and will be more dedicated to making it work. This would be the ideal situation, but remember this should be a starting point. If the market is not showing demand for your idea, nix it. On the other hand, if the market seems to like the topic you are passionate about, focus on creating apps in that area.

How do you know if the market wants your app? Just look at the top app charts. Are apps like the ones you want to do listed there? If yes, you've got a potential winner. If not, keep looking. It's that simple.

When you follow in the footsteps of successful apps, you will have a better chance of succeeding because these apps have proven demand and an existing user base. This takes the guesswork out of creating app ideas.

I can't stress enough the importance of emulating existing apps. It's easy for people to fall in love with their own idea even if the market doesn't show an appetite for it. This is one of the most costly mistakes you can make.

Developers make this mistake all the time. They focus on generating original ideas and spend a lot of time and effort creating those apps. When it doesn't work, instead of learning from the market, they go to the next untested idea. Often times, they repeat this cycle until they run out of money and are frustrated with the app game. This doesn't have to be your experience.

One example of an app that seemed to be a great idea, but didn't do so well is the Pocket Dream Girl app. (See Figure 4.1.) It was created by a friend of mine, and the premise behind it was that the user can create

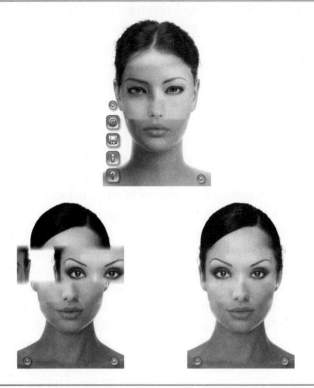

FIGURE 4.1   Pocket Dream Girl.

the face of his dream girl by mixing and matching the hair, eyes, nose, and mouth of over 20 women. As a result, the user could create over 150,000 *Weird Science*-type women.

When I heard the idea, I thought it was a good app and that it could work. Before starting development, I would have researched the market, realized no demand for this type of app existed, and moved on. But my friend was in love with his idea and had the app developed without being discerning or doing any market research. It was nicely done, but as you can imagine, the app flopped.

You want to avoid this mistake with your apps, and if you listen to the market, you will.

Another trap to watch for is being sidetracked by others. In my experience, the first rule of making cash as an appreneur is to stick to your game plan, and avoid advice from anyone who hasn't had any success in the app business. Generally, your friends, family, and peers will think they are experts in the industry. Most will even graciously help you with new ideas to guarantee you have a money-making concept.

However, I've always found this enthusiasm distracting. Other people's advice is usually based on fantasies of striking it rich, with minimal market research in the form of their girlfriends, their cousins, or their parole officer. I can't tell you how many times I've heard people tell me, "That will make you so much money!" or, "I have the best app idea. You have to do it; you're going to be rich!"

While support from others can be encouraging, don't let it cloud your judgment, or you will be sure to catch the empty pocket syndrome. Treat family and friends as who they are: consumers. Let them test your apps and give feedback as a user, especially if they are in your demographic. Don't, however, take business advice from them if they haven't proven themselves to be successful in this industry.

Taking their advice is an easy trap to fall into because whenever people ask you "What do you do?" you'll unintentionally invite lots of questions, advice, and suggestions since everyone is interested in this exciting industry. Everybody has their own million-dollar idea and will be sure to make you listen to it. Be discerning, stick to your game plan, and stay focused on your idea from concept to development. Allow yourself to be swayed in a new direction based on facts and objective data and not by one person's subjective opinion.

STOP HATIN', START EMULATIN'

Emulating competitors is one of the most fundamental concepts in business. When Apple launched the first iPod in 2001, MP3 players weren't anything new. The first mainstream MP3 music player entered the market three years before the iPod came along. The iPod became a massive success because it was sleek, intuitive, and fun.

The iPhone wasn't the first smartphone, but Apple saw a need for more innovative features, and took smartphones to the next level as it did with MP3 players. With focus on the consumer and beautiful design, Apple made the iPod and iPhone the game-changing successes they are today.

Facebook is notorious for recognizing something that works, making it better, and adapting it into its platform. Facebook offers integrated e-mail, newsfeeds, instant messaging, video chat, and apps. You can get

FIGURE 4.2   No need to reinvent the wheel.

each of these somewhere else, but they're more fun or easier to use on Facebook.

The find-something-that-works-and-make-it-better philosophy has been around since the beginning of time. Thank God, because if that wasn't the case, we might still be swinging from branches and picking our butts.

> My friends Michael Moon and Quoc Bui make $80,000 to $100,000 a month on the App Store with their company FreeTheApps. Michael always says, "Don't be discouraged if you see that your idea has already been done. That just means that there is a market for your idea, and if anything, this should be encouragement!"

Some of the greatest app ideas are improvements on an existing app or a twist on an old idea, taking it in a fresh, new direction. The story of Smack Talk and the series of Talking Friends apps is a perfect example of the idea of emulation at work.

Smack Talk was an app that became successful in the early days of the App Store. (See Figure 4.3.) The app portrays cute, little animals repeating whatever you say but in a high-pitched voice. It was an intuitive, innovative, first of its kind, incredibly entertaining app. Seriously, who wouldn't love a little hamster sounding like someone who had inhaled helium repeating your own words?

Smack Talk stayed on the top charts for quite some time and was a sensation. This was a great accomplishment for a great app. Many developers

FIGURE 4.3   Smack Talk.

followed this app in awe, wishing it was their idea. They didn't dare to compete because trying to surpass such a successful app seemed like fighting a losing battle. They accepted that this genre had been cornered by Smack Talk and continued with business as usual.

However, a company called Outfit7 had other plans. It didn't hesitate to compete and take the concept to a new level. It made a variant of the application called Talking Tom (Figure 4.4), which included the basic voice playback feature in addition to a 3D interactive cartoonish cat. The user was entertained through the voice playback and could enjoy a new set of features such as the ability to touch the cat and get a reaction. The app offered new ways of interacting, more animation, and brilliant marketing.

Talking Tom overtook Smack Talk in 2010, but Outfit7 pressed on to create an entire suite of Talking Friends apps with lots of different animals.

FIGURE 4.4   Talking Tom.

This made Outfit7 a multimillion-dollar company and one of the most successful app companies to date. Its apps have been downloaded over 200 million times and have consistently appeared in the top 100 paid and free apps overall.

Who would've thought that a well-developed and successful app could be taken to such new heights? These opportunities are all over the App Store waiting to be discovered.

If you're just starting out, stick to creating apps in areas that have high demand. Find something that a large group of people, from teenagers to adults, can find useful or fun instead of catering to a niche group. Stick to low-risk, high-probability apps.

Does this mean you should never be innovative and try something that hasn't been done before?

Actually, yes. Well, sort of . . .

LEARN FROM EXISTING APPS

Most inexperienced apprenuers spend far too much of their time trying to be original, when what they are looking for is right in front of them.

I'm not suggesting you copy another developer's app, but your first step should be to get curious and see what other successful developers are doing. You should spend time figuring out why their apps work, read user reviews, and collect data.

Whenever you decide to look into emulating an app, ask yourself these six questions:

1. Why are people purchasing this?
2. Can I do something to emulate this idea and take it to another level?
3. What other apps would this app's demographic like?
4. How many other similar apps are in the market? (Go to appempire .com/topappcharts to find out.)
5. How successful and consistent have they been?
6. How does their marketing and pricing model work?

When you look at all the top lists, think about which applications you would genuinely consider downloading. Why do you like them, and what stands out about them?

Think about how to take the same concept to the next level while continuing to attract the same demographic. Write what improvements you would make. Would you add a new feature? Change the look? Add better graphics and marketing? How would you give users more value?

Look at more than one competitor. Download all of the successful competitors of this app. Learn what these apps do right and where they fall short. Decide whether you can do this better, while incorporating what your audience is asking for.

I see this happening on the App Store on a consistent basis, and here is a recent example of how I put the power of emulating other apps into action.

After the Apple ranking algorithm change, I started noticing a shift in app rankings. During my daily research, I saw that some apps that had rarely appeared in the top charts, like emoticon apps, were starting to rise in the rankings. I love using those emoticons and wanted to do an Emoji app, but until that time, I had not seen the market get too excited about them. Also, most Emoji apps are simple and are used only once: to unlock the Emoji keyboard.

With the markets interest increasing, I decided to take a closer look and downloaded all the major emoticon apps. I liked what I saw, but I noticed the apps had limited functionality. How could my app be better than a competitor's if the Emoji keyboard had a limited number of emoticons that could not be increased? How lucrative could an app be if it is used once? I think most other developers would have allowed these limitations to stop them from pursuing this idea, but I've always been stubborn and this time it paid off.

So, I kept brainstorming until it hit me. If I could not add more smileys to the Emoji keyboard, then why not include a bunch of smileys within the app that people could send as images via text messages, emails, or any other medium that could handle images? With that in mind, I created an app that unlocked the Emoji keyboard and added value with more than 450 additional smileys, which could be shared via SMS, e-mail, Facebook, and so on. This became more fun for users because they had more smileys to send to their friends. The app was used constantly since users had to return to the app to send an emoticon. (See Figure 4.5.)

This Emoji app was developed in two weeks. It followed the freemium model, meaning free, with an in-app purchase option. The app hit the number one spot in the App Store's productivity category and the number 12 spot in the top free overall category within six days, raking in nearly $500 a day. BINGO.

The process I went through is simple and you can repeat it easily. Why make things harder than they have to be? The market is putting up its hand saying, "Hey! Look at me," telling you what it likes. Be sure to listen up and cash in.

Once you've made a bunch of money, you can try apps that are outside the norm because you can market them with your app network even if they don't do too well on their own. Until then, focus on iteration, not innovation.

NARROWING DOWN YOUR IDEAS

As you do your research, make sure to capture the top app ideas you would like to emulate. You might have a bunch of ideas and not know which one to focus on, but don't worry because this is normal. One

FIGURE 4.5 Emoji screenshots.

way of simplifying things is to remember from Chapter 3 that only two types of apps exist: entertainment and utility. You can always focus on one of these first if it makes your task simpler.

Let's go through the process of assessing your app ideas. First, write down up to five of your most promising ideas based on your research. If you don't have any yet, why not check out the App Store to see if you can find some inspiration.

My Top Five App Ideas

1.
2.
3.
4.
5.

Assess your ideas based on the traits checklist I showed you in Chapter 3. Here it is again. For each one of your app ideas, check each one of the eight traits it has.

1. Fun/Entertaining
2. Intuitive
3. Engaging
4. Addictive
5. Valuable
6. Cross-Cultural
7. Great Graphics/Sounds
8. Viral

The more of these you can check off, the better your chance will be to create a successful app. I usually check each one of these but might go for an idea that is missing one or two. Cross out any apps that have fewer than six traits, and go back to the drawing board. Keep going through this exercise until you have three ideas that meet six or more of these traits.

Something else to keep in mind, when picking your top three, is the App Store review guidelines. These rules are used by Apple during the review process, and if you don't follow them, your app will be rejected. For example, you may have seen the plethora of fart or flashlight apps on the App Store. As a result, Apple has decided to no longer accept those types of apps. Knowing these rules can save you a lot of time and effort. If you see any of your ideas conflicting with the guidelines, reject them and move on to the next one.

Make sure to go through this exercise now or at the end of this chapter. We're going to get quotes for your top three ideas once you find developers using the methods in the next chapter.

TIMING IS EVERYTHING

Another crucial component when it comes to deciding what app idea to go with is timing. Because the market doesn't seem to be ready for your idea at the moment doesn't mean that this won't change in the future.

For example, during rehab, I found yoga to be incredible for regaining my range of motion. I became passionate about it and thought about creating an app for other yogis. I went onto appempire.com/topappcharts and searched for "yoga." That was around November 2009.

I found that none of the yoga apps ranked high in the top charts, even in the health and fitness category. Even though I was passionate about yoga, I had to listen to the data. The market wasn't big enough for the app.

More than two years later, in August 2011, I saw that a yoga app ranked second in the health and fitness category. At that point, the market had grown enough for me to consider spending time on a yoga app.

If I had created a yoga app two years earlier, could I have made money with it? Sure, but the probability of the app being successful would have been low due to low visibility. Yes, timing is everything.

Similarly, as you can be too early for the market, you can also be too late. Make sure that you don't get analysis paralysis. At some point, it will be time to execute. If you see something that you think will work, strike immediately. App ideas can have a limited window of opportunity and you don't want to miss that. You want to launch your app while the market you're watching is still hot.

TAKING SMALL STEPS

Here is a million-dollar question: You have $25,000. You have the option to create one app that takes five months to develop and costs $25,000 or 10 apps that each take two weeks to develop and cost $2,500 each. Which strategy should you follow? Sadly, most developers choose the first route. They think they have an amazing idea, and spend a lot of time and money on it. This is too risky because no matter how you select your app ideas, you won't know if they will be accepted until you test them in the marketplace.

My app strategy has been to create straightforward, low-cost apps that are in the same ballpark as those with proven success in the market. The only way to know if your idea is successful is to test it in the market. You need to find out if customers have an appetite for your idea, and if you can get the marketing right before you spend too much money and add everything but the kitchen sink to it. You can upgrade and add features after the market embraces your product and you have a better understanding of the app's demographic and longevity.

The best way to test the market is to launch a free app first. A free app usually costs less because typically it has fewer features. It's cost-effective and has the lowest barrier to entry for consumers because it's free. After all if you can't give away your app for free, how are you going to make people pay for it? Don't worry, there's plenty of money to be made from a free app even when you're testing the market. In Chapter 9, I'll explain how.

Make sure you can create your app as cost effectively as possible, without skimping on graphics or core functionality. If you can't develop your current idea at a reasonable price, shelve it, and go with your other ideas first.

As you've seen in this chapter, a method behind the madness exists for picking hit app ideas. It's a repeatable process, and the more you use it the better you will become. Now that you have all these ideas, it's time to look for developers who can turn them into reality.

What I Learned

1.
2.
3.

Actions to Take

1. Look at the market and make a list of apps you would like to emulate.
2. Look at apps similar to the ones you want to develop to see how consistently successful they have been. Is the market hungry for this?
3. See if there's a way you can improve the functionality and marketing of an existing successful app to give more value for the customer.
4. Pick your best three ideas based on your research, Apple guidelines, and timing considerations.

You're the Brains and They're the Brawn

How to Hire Great Programmers

Coming together is a beginning, staying together is progress, and working together is success.

—Henry Ford

"Wait, wait wait. How do you expect to create an app if you're not a programmer?" His words pierced through my superficial layers of confidence and left me feeling confused, speechless, and wondering the same thing.

I responded with a quick, defensive, "Hire someone, of course."

Without a skip of a beat he immediately followed with, "Okay. Well, how do you find those people?"

Again my answer was less than smooth. I remember becoming frustrated and wishing I hadn't bragged about my million-dollar app idea in the waiting room of my doctor's office to an 88-year-old man who didn't even know what an iPhone was. Nevertheless, he was right, and I didn't have the slightest clue what I was talking about. I figured there had to be a way, and I was going to turn over every rock I could to find the answer.

Later that day, I boarded a plane back to Vermont to continue my recovery at my family's house. Fueled by my frustrations with the conversation earlier in the day, I bought a fresh copy of *Macworld,* a magazine about all things Apple, hoping to gain some insight about apps. I started flipping through it and landed on a quarter page ad that read "TURN YOUR APP IDEA INTO $$$." It was an ad from a software development company that was offering iPhone app development services. Jackpot. *I will show you, you cynical waiting room critic,* I thought to myself.

Meanwhile, as I was taking in every bit of information the ad had to offer, the pilot had started his "Ladies and gentleman, blah blah, thank you for flying with us, blah blah" spiel. When I was done with the ad and looked up full of excitement, he was completing his announcement, with "Sit back, relax, and enjoy the ride." Little did I know that his words were not only meant for that plane ride but also for my app adventure, which was about to take off.

A few days later, I found out that the development company in the magazine was located only two hours away from where I was staying in Vermont. At the time, I still had the old-school real estate mentality that business had to be done in person. So, I decided to take a trip down to have a face-to-face meeting with them.

"Nice to meet you," John, the owner, said as I shook hands with him and the team. Their eyes were glued on me, which made me feel completely out of place. *Maybe this wasn't a good idea*, I thought to myself. My inner Negative Nancy was chiming in. I awkwardly sat down at their board-room table, and started telling them my idea and how I knew nothing about this new world of apps but that I was eager to learn.

"No worries. We will help you out," said Kevin, the project manager. After a few minutes discussing how the app would work, how long it would take, and how much it would cost, my uneasiness drifted away and I began to feel more confident.

I left the office that sunny Friday afternoon with my head held high and a swagger in my step. Talking to them had given me clarity and removed many of the hurdles I had seen before me. That's when I understood the importance of what development companies do and the value they can bring to an app business. Suddenly I believed almost anything was possible in the app world. My brain opened up and my thoughts turned into an uncontrollable creative avalanche. The possibilities seemed endless. "Okay, we can do this, and we can do that." I started coming up with all kinds of ideas and I actually had the people to execute them. Problem solved. Next.

As an appreneur, it's easy to hit a barrier because you may not know if the technology will support your app ideas. The great thing about programmers is they can give you answers. Instead of blocking your creativity, hire the right people and be resourceful. I lucked out with my first development team, and then through multiple experiences, some good and some bad, I learned how to hire good people. In this chapter, you will learn how to find, hire, manage, and fire developers and to set up systems that will help you turn your possibilities into realities.

THE IMPORTANCE OF PROGRAMMERS

As of this chapter, you have been researching the market on a regular basis and have used the last chapter to create up to three well thought-out app ideas. Now what? If you are a programmer or are technically inclined you might think "Cool, I can write my own apps" or "I'll teach myself how to code an app." You might get a few books on how to program and start writing code at crazy hours of the night hooked up to an IV full of coffee.

Well, you could do that but I would highly advise against it. It's important that you keep your momentum and get an app out to the market as soon as possible. Coding your own app, especially if you're teaching yourself at the same time, will take too long. The likelihood of you getting stuck and giving up is very high.

This model will also be unsustainable over the long run when you want to create several apps at the same time and consistently update your existing apps. After all, the idea is to get your time back and escape the long hours of the rat race.

Another reason to outsource app development is that you have to focus on the role of a businessowner. This means having a bird's-eye view of key aspects of your business like market research, marketing, networking, and so on. You won't be able to do that if you're spending all your time in the trenches. You don't see Donald Trump running around with a hard hat on the 40th floor of his new skyscraper and hammering in nails do you?

You must decide that you will focus on the high-level operations of your company rather than getting lost in executing minute details. Programmers will be the foundation of your business and allow you to create apps quickly and scale easily, which will allow you to remain the captain of your ship.

WHAT TO LOOK FOR IN PROGRAMMERS

Since programmers play such a vital role in your business, you must be particularly discerning when it comes to selecting them. Just as you wouldn't let anyone build your dream home, you need to use care with who is laying the virtual bricks of your mobile empire.

When it comes to selecting programmers, you have to focus on certain key areas. These include experience, communication, team, pricing, and conflict of interest.

Experience

The first thing you need to assess is the programmer's level of experience. It's not a good idea to work with programmers who haven't worked on many apps. Sometimes when programmers are beginning, they will offer cheap rates. This is like taking a helicopter ride with a pilot who has only flown a few times. I wouldn't recommend it.

One of the first things I ask to see when considering new programmers is the apps they have created. If a picture speaks a thousand words, to me, an app speaks 10 thousand. Download the programmers' apps and assess the quality of the work. Does it look sharp and work flawlessly, or is it clumsy? Does it look professional or substandard?

Sometimes they are bound by nondisclosure agreements (NDAs) and are not able to disclose the apps they have worked on, or they have only worked on parts of an app. Regardless of this, you have to see their products in action. If you can't, move on unless you're into buying cars without test-driving them.

The programmer's website can be a useful assessment tool. This is particularly true for development companies, which often showcase their work on their website. It should highlight some of the apps they've done and give you confidence they aren't a fly-by-night company. The quality of the website can indicate the quality of apps they create. Independent programmers don't always have a nice website, but if their portfolio of apps is impressive, you should continue assessing them.

When hiring a programmer, ask for references. Talk to at least one person who has worked with this programmer before. I prefer two or three, which can be difficult to get, but why not try? This is not as important for programmers that you find on outsourcing websites, such as oDesk (appempire.com/odesk) or Freelancer (appempire.com/freelancer). On these sites, assessing developers is easier because you can review detailed statistics on their previous work performance. You will see reviews and ratings from their previous clients and can determine if they're somebody you would want to work with.

After doing a general assessment of the programmers' skills, you need to ensure they have the specific experience necessary to complete the app. I get into this usually during a second conversation after I've done my initial assessment and had the programmer sign an NDA. You will be able to estimate the skill level when you look at the previous work, but you still have to make sure that the programmer has the specific skills your app requires.

Communication

Even though cost of development in other countries may be lower, the language barrier can be a hassle. Work with programmers who share your native language. You must be able to communicate with your developer effectively. It may cost more, but you will get higher quality work and fewer headaches. Does this mean you should never work with somebody from another country? Of course not, but just make sure they're fluent in your language.

Something else I expect from programmers is technical guidance. When I started, I was a complete novice, but I was fortunate to work with programmers who educated me about technical jargon during the entire process. Not all programmers are skilled at this even if they're good at creating applications. Make sure your first programmers are willing and able to explain things to you in non-technical terms.

As you gain experience in the field, you will need less guidance, but initially this is important. You will find out quickly if you are talking to programmers who do this inherently. They will ask you questions and often give you a crash course to help you understand the scope of the application you want to create. This is huge. Programmers should not be your only source of education, therefore rely on yourself as well to learn what is necessary for this business.

Another big one is responsiveness. You've had a peek at how fast-paced this industry is. Sometimes a delay of a week can make a difference of a few thousand dollars. You must be able to make changes on the fly, therefore you need programmers who are as responsive as possible. If you're dealing with programmers who have too much on their plate, find people who can make you their priority. Keep an eye on the programmers' responsiveness at all times, especially during projects. Don't allow for any lapses, and mention problems if you see them.

By the way, this is true for yourself as well. Programmers are people like you and me, and they can get frustrated if they feel their time is wasted. If they need something from you, get it to them quickly. Be as responsive as you expect them to be. In the beginning, I was notorious for not getting my programmers what they needed and often created bottlenecks and delays.

Also, silence your inner control freak and do not be too high maintenance. You have to stay on top of things but excessive communication will slow down and possibly frustrate the programmers. I usually ask them how often they like to talk about the project. Come up with a schedule that accommodates both of you and stick to it.

Another important step is being cautious of working with programmers in different time zones. Keep the time difference to a minimum because it can become a major hiccup in communication. Maintaining the momentum of your business will be difficult if by the time you get up in the morning your programmer has hit stage three of his sleep cycle.

One of the most brilliant programmers I've worked with before lives in Germany, and whenever I'm on the West Coast, the nine-hour difference makes it almost impossible for us to work together. When he closes shop at 5 p.m., it's 8 a.m. here. Of course, he can make exceptions at times, but this is unsustainable. Some outsourcing companies rearrange their employees' workday to match it to the U.S. workday, but if you don't have at least a three- to four-hour window of shared time, find someone else.

Team

Whenever possible, work with a team rather than an individual especially in the beginning. This has several advantages. Teams can be more reliable since they can pick up the slack if the programmer working on your project gets sick or becomes unavailable. This is a big one as you can imagine. Ensure that not everything rests on one person's shoulders especially as your projects become more complex.

A bigger team can get things done faster. App development can't always be evenly distributed among a set number of people, but a skilled team will know how to get things done faster without losing track of the overall project.

The biggest reason for using a team is that a team will include graphics designers and sometimes project managers. You can have the best code in the world, but if your graphics look bad, people will be less likely to give your app a chance. The ideal situation would be to have a programmer who can code and create the graphics. This is rare, so the second-best option is having programmers and graphic designers working in tandem, like a well-oiled machine. You will also use graphics to market your apps, so having a graphic designer who can create killer marketing materials is a must.

One more benefit of working with a team is the variety in the programmers' skill sets. Initially you will want to have the right talent for your first app. But as you create a greater variety of apps, you might reach the limits of a programmer's abilities. Your programmer should be able to reach out to his team members or his professional network for assistance.

These are guidelines and not strict rules. As you gain more experience, special circumstances may warrant using a programmer who does not work with a team or have graphics capabilities but has a specific skill set that you need. Keep this to a minimum because it's easier and less risky to have everything under one roof.

Pricing

You can expect a wide range of prices and services since many companies and independent developers compete for your business. Projects can be billed at a fixed cost or hourly rate.

Start with contractors who offer a flat fee, with a certain number of free refinements (called *iterations*). I rarely develop apps on an hourly rate because I feel programmers don't have an incentive to finish fast. I want them to feel the same sense of urgency that I do when it comes to developing apps. Being on an hourly rate has the opposite effect. This is not true for all developers, but this strategy has served me well and has become my preference based on my experiences. If people have done some quality work for you in the past, and they prefer hourly rates, that might be the way to go for you.

Another advantage of fixed-rate projects is that it'll be much easier to stay within your budget if you know how much the work will cost. You want to get as many apps to the market as possible with your initial budget. Going for fixed-rate projects might mean the difference between creating two apps versus one.

You might ask, "How do I know that I'm getting a fair quote for my app?" Typically, companies are going to charge more because they have more overhead than individual programmers. You can avoid overpaying by getting quotes from three different developers for each one of your ideas. Discrepancies will exist between the prices, and as you figure out why, you will learn a tremendous amount about the programmers and about your app. Don't be afraid to tell programmers you prefer that you have other quotes that are lower than theirs (only if this is true, of course). They might match it. Business 101.

As for payment, you should never pay upfront in full. Avoid a down payment if you can, but if you can't, ask the programmer to provide clear milestones and prices for each of them. Don't release a payment until you're confident the requirements of the milestone have been met. The nice thing about sites like oDesk and Freelancer is that they mitigate the payment process by acting as an escrow service and providing a payment system that corollates with the milestones.

Be cautious about using royalty agreements when it comes to paying for apps. Some developers will lower their development cost if they receive a cut of the app's income (called royalties). It's easy to think, "Oh, giving up 10 or 20 percent is not a big deal." You might save money or the programmers may do a better job if they are vested, but these advantages are negligible to the potential disadvantages of a royalty deal.

A royalty deal essentially makes the programmers your business partner, which can get messy. What if you want changes to the app they disagree with? Or what if they interfere with your marketing efforts? What happens if you have an opportunity to sell the app or your company? An app can be a long-term asset and giving up a piece of it can take away a lot of money. Keeping track of royalty payments can be cumbersome as well.

Conflict of Interest

Sometimes programmers create their own apps and publish them on the App Store. Their hope is they might strike gold, but in the meantime, they will make extra cash by developing apps for others. These will mostly be independent developers, but some development companies do this as well.

Strictly speaking, this is a conflict of interest because your competition is creating your products. This is so prevalent in the industry that you probably won't be able to avoid it. Just be protected as much as possible by showing the programmers your awareness of this and have them sign NDAs and possibly app-specific non-compete agreements. But don't let this prevent you from moving forward.

FINDING AND SELECTING PROGRAMMERS

When I started my company in early 2009, the industry was so new that it was hard to find quality programmers. Because of the worldwide app craze, you can now find them more easily. Many software development companies now focus on app development. Quite a few independent programmers have appeared all over the place.

For my first few apps, I found it much easier to work with a well-known company that could hold my hand before diving in with independent programmers. This was a good starting point because the company was versed in working with inexperienced clients. I recommend you go the same route because bigger companies have more experience with educating people who are wet behind the ears. This will help you accelerate your learning the basics of app development and teach you how to communicate with programmers. Working with this company gave me the confidence and momentum I needed to continue to forge ahead in the app business.

How do you look for programmers? Well, you have many ways to look for programmers such as a simple Google search, job sites like Monster, Craigslist, app conferences, meet-up groups, programmer forums, word of mouth, and outsourcing sites (such as oDesk and Freelancer). Some of these methods are easier than others, but no magic formula exists. You'll have to use various sources and assess multiple programmers until you find several who you're comfortable pulling the trigger with.

Your approach will basically be the same with each programmer or company you're assessing. Once you have programmers on the phone or on Skype, interview them until you're comfortable with moving to the quoting step. This is a job interview, and you're the boss. Here is my question checklist:

- How long have you been developing apps?
- How many apps have you worked on?
- Can I see the apps you've worked on?
- Do you have a website? What is it?
- Do you have references I can talk to?
- Whats your schedule like? How soon can you start?
- How long will it take to get a quote?
- What's our time difference? (if they are in a different time zone)
- What time do you usually work? What are your hours?
- What's frustrating for you when working with clients?
- Are you working with a team? What are their skills?
- Can you create graphics, or do you have somebody who can?
- Can I see examples of the graphics work?
- What happens if you become sick during a project?
- What if you hit a technical hurdle during the project? Do you have other team members or a network of programmers who can help you?
- Can you provide flat-fee quotes?
- What's your payment schedule?

- Can you create milestones tied to payments?
- Do you publish your own apps on the App Store?
- How do you ensure that you don't compete with your clients?
- How do you submit an app to the App Store? (Can they walk you through, or do they make you feel brain challenged?)

This list will change based on whom you're talking to. An established development company will most likely have a team of developers and graphics people on staff but you must get answers to the above questions before moving forward. Also, you don't need to sound like a drill sergeant or ask silly interview questions. The questions listed above are important, and they shouldn't make the person you're talking to defensive if you ask them in a friendly tone. I always have this question list in front of me during an interview and take notes as I get the responses. I've found that, in business conversations, it's good to throw some personality in there and have a little fun. Keep this in mind when you're asking your questions.

During the conversation, pay attention to how well they were able to explain themselves. Were they articulate? Did they use too much techno babble? Did they actually speak the same language? Did they seem confident with their answers? How was their tone and demeanor? If you had any issues or worries, you may want to move on to somebody else. If you can communicate with them and your gut is telling you yes, you'll want to move to the next step.

In either case, thank them for their time and mention that you will follow with an NDA agreement if you decide to move forward. Don't give away your ideas during this initial conversation. Whenever the topic comes up, say you'll be more than happy to discuss everything after they sign the NDA. You must protect your ideas, source code, and any other intellectual property because these are your assets.

Be careful with the people who handle your code as well. As your business grows, you will not only be creating new apps but also maintaining your existing ones. This means you'll have to give your code to whoever has to make changes to it. Only do this after you have established a certain level of trust. This is especially true with your popular apps.

Once the NDA is in place, it's time to dive in and ensure the developers have the skill to complete your app. You do not have any wiggle room here, especially for your first app. Either they know how to do it or they don't. You want to hear things like, "I know exactly how to do that" or

"I've done similar apps, so it will not be a problem." You don't want to hear things like, "I should be able to do that, but I have to research a few things" or "I'm not sure but I can probably figure it out." If you hear those words, move to an app they are confident about or run for the hills.

For example, let's say you're developing a new app with sophisticated audio requirements. You could find great programmers who have done lots of apps, but they would be a bad choice if they have never worked with audio before. Use them for their expertise for some of your other apps and find somebody else for the audio app.

As you're going through this entire process, you will be getting feedback on their responsiveness. If it's taking too long for them to sign the NDA and to clarify things, this might indicate how slowly the development process will move.

Using outsourcing websites can be a great tool to find skilled, low-cost programmers. These websites allow programmers to bid on jobs that you post. As you can imagine, the competition creates a bidding frenzy that gives you a good chance of getting quality work at a low price. Following are three of the top outsourcing sites (see Figure 5.1):

1. **oDesk (appempire.com/odesk)**—Its work diary feature tracks the hours your programmer is working for you and takes screenshots of the programmer's desktop at certain time intervals. You can review these images to know the programmer was working on your project and not participating in his local dodgeball championship.

2. **Freelancer (appempire.com/freelancer)**—This site has the most programmers listed. They claim that twice as many programmers will respond to your ad, and I found this to be mostly true.

3. **Guru/Elance (appempire.com/guru - appempire.com/elance)**—These sites have large lists of programmers, and it's always good to have different pools of talent competing for your business.

Here are the advantages and disadvantages of these sites.

Advantages:

- **Lots of programmers**—These sites have large databases of programmers competing for your project.
- **Fast responses**—You often get bids within an hour or two of your posting.

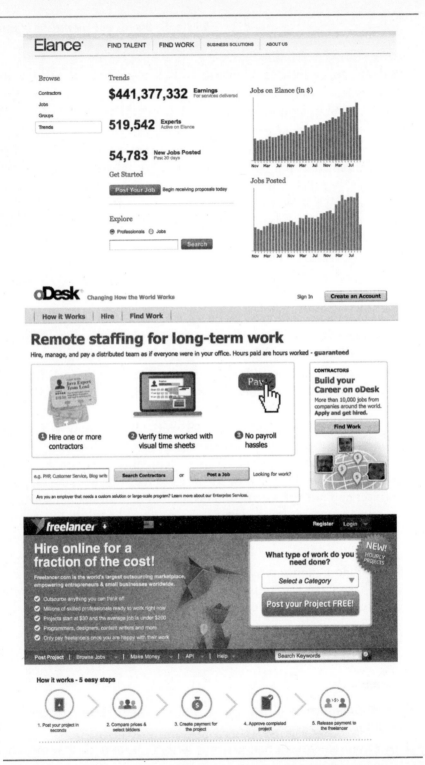

FIGURE 5.1 Screenshots of Elance, oDesk, and freelancer.

- **Skill and work history**—Programmers have profiles that list their skills. You can review the previous projects they have worked on. With this information, you can evaluate if they have the specific skills for your app.
- **Performance rating and reviews**—Clients can rate and review the programmer. You'll know if it's worth spending more time assessing the person.
- **Price comparison**—Before posting your job, you can review active and closed job listings of others to get an idea for what others have paid for apps similar to yours.
- **Escrow services**—Your funds are protected and you only release them at certain milestones if you're happy with the work.

Disadvantages:

- **Communication**—Most of these programmers are overseas. This can present issues with communication and time zone differences, so a Skype interview is an absolute must before you continue.
- **Protecting your idea**—Because these sites are public bidding grounds, your ideas can get hijacked. When posting a job, never post your idea or marketing plan. Use general descriptions until you have an NDA.

Here are five pointers on posting a job on oDesk and assessing the responses. The process is similar on the other sites. Your ad should cast a wide net to attract as many applicants as possible. You can filter later.

1. **Enter the skill requirements**—What programming languages do they know? Odesk and Freelancer allow you to list up to five. This way only programmers with those skills will receive your job post. For iPhone apps, the skills I use are iPhone, Objective C, Cocoa, and C Programming.
2. **Give a basic description of your project**—Keep it simple and skill-specific. Tell the applicants that you will discuss details during the selection process.
3. **Post your ad only for a few days**—This way programmers have a sense of urgency to quickly bid on your job.
4. **Filter applicants**—I always filter applicants using these criteria:
   - They have a rating of four or five stars.
   - They have at least 100 hours of work logged.
   - Their English is good.

5. **Compose a message to all suitable applicants**—This message invites the applicant to a Skype call for further screening. Disqualify anyone who is not willing to jump a Skype call.

As you interview more programmers (regardless of where you find them) you'll get skilled at finding the talented ones. Even if a programmer passes all your tests, trust your gut because it's usually right.

HOW TO CONVEY YOUR IDEA

When I began working with programmers, I would explain to them what kind of app I wanted and how it should work. I thought I was being clear and was surprised when I received products that weren't close to my vision. It would take several iterations and a lot of time and frustration to fix things. I was even getting upset at the programmers at times, but it turned out it wasn't their fault. It was mine. I wasn't communicating accurately and was making the process frustrating for both of us. Once I realized what the problem was, everything changed. Projects were completed much faster and everybody was happier.

To convey my idea properly, I draw it on a piece of paper. Maybe it will look like a three-year-old's artwork, but it will still convey what you're trying to do. Some people like putting this together in digital form on their computer. Whatever you're most comfortable with and whatever gives the programmers the details they need is the way to go.

To make things easier, I look at certain apps in the App Store, and reference them to more accurately show my programmers what I'm looking for. For example, I'll say, "Download the XYZ app. I want the ABC functionality to work like theirs. Take a look at the screenshots from this other app, and change this." I take certain components of apps that I'd like to emulate, and give them to the programmer so that we are as clear as possible.

The clearer you are, the fewer misunderstandings and problems you will have. The idea is to convey what the app will look like, where everything will be placed, and what happens if certain buttons are selected. This helps the programmer know what you want and is a useful tool when designing your app. Do not be vague or ambiguous. You should know what every part of your app will do. If you don't, you need to develop your idea more thoroughly. The programmer will be unable to deliver what you want if you are uncertain what that is.

When I send the sketch to the programmer, I arrange a meeting over Skype. My sketch usually is as detailed as possible but inevitably the programmer has questions or points out flaws or technical hurdles. We talk it out, and we ensure we understand how every screen, button, and feature is going to work and look. This can take several iterations before we get it right. Programmers shouldn't write a single line of code until the design is finalized.

This is part of figuring out the app's complexity and functionality. As programmers quote different features, they often give you new ideas that can improve your apps. You don't want to add too many extra features in the beginning due to cost and time but you never know when you might get a free gold nugget worth including. Sometimes you will find your idea is impossible and can move on without wasting too much time.

You have to consider the design to be final once the coding begins. You will have ideas for additional features as you start testing the initial versions of your app. Changing things after some work has been done can frustrate a programmer. It's like telling your builder who has installed your fireplace that you want it on the other side of the living room. That will not go over too well. Most people don't realize this is what they are demanding of their programmer when they ask for major changes. That's why you should take your time planning the app during the design and why the quoting process is important.

On the other hand, you can't anticipate every question that may arise during development, and you may have to change your design. This is normal and programmers expect this to a certain degree. Nonetheless, don't make major changes that negate days or weeks of work and put your team on edge.

If you keep adding features, you might unnecessarily increase costs and production time. You need to get the app to the market quickly and in a basic form to test the market. Only redesign during coding if you feel you have a good justification for this. Otherwise, add the idea to your update list and move forward with the development. I have an update list for each app and refer back to it when I want to make additions to one of my apps.

When I use this design process, many times the first version of an app is about 90 percent of the final, and we need only one or two more iterations to finalize the work. Depending on your experience, your initial layouts will probably not be totally on point, but as you learn the ropes and get a couple of apps under your belt, you will be able to create clearer designs.

The best part is the programmers can give me accurate quotes if they understand the scope of the project. This will help you, especially when you're getting started and you're on a tight budget.

TESTING HIRED PROGRAMMERS

Now it's time to get quotes and test the candidates. I recommend going to three different programmers to get quotes for each one of your three ideas. Most people think they have to invest a lot of money to create a hit app. To give you an idea of my initial start-up costs with my first app, I paid the developer $1,800 and the return on that investment was in the six figures. Pricing will vary based on the app but, keep your initial development costs as low as possible. As you gain more experience and are making money, you can safely move up to higher cost projects.

At this point, you have found programmers, screened them, signed NDAs, conveyed your ideas, received a few quotes, and picked the ones to work with. Rather than jumping into a full-fledged project with both feet, I usually test them on something small first. I systematically ask for these three things every time I'm working with a new programmer:

1. **Icon**—Ask the programmer to create and deliver the icon of the app. Figure 5.2 is the picture you see when you are looking at an app on iTunes or on your phone. After you have outlined your app idea, you will probably have several ideas for icons as well. Pass these on and ask for a finished 512 × 512 iTunes Artwork version of the icon. They will know what that means.

2. **Hello, World! app**—Ask the programmer for a "Hello, World!" app. This will take them 10 minutes to create and is a simple app that opens up and shows a page that displays "Hello, World!" (See Figure 5.3.) Programmers will know what this is. The idea here is not to test their programming skills but to determine how they will deliver apps to you for testing. This app should include the icons so you can see how it will look on your phone.

3. **App Delivery**—When the programmers are ready to show you a test version of your app, they have to create something called an "ad hoc." This ad hoc version of your app needs to be installed on your phone before you can test it. The installation process was

FIGURE 5.2 App icons.

FIGURE 5.3   Hello, World!

FIGURE 5.4   TestFlight service.

a bit cumbersome in the past but a new service called TestFlight has simplified this process (appempire.com/testflightapp, see Figure 5.4). I ask all programmers to use this service even if they have not used it before. They will be able to figure it out, and you'll be able to install your test apps with a few touches on your phone.

I never spend more than a couple of hundred dollars, but this test helps me see the graphics capabilities, implementation speed, and overall work dynamic (such as communication and time zone). You want to start off on the right foot or get out quickly if you need to, and this is the best way to do it.

Mention that you like to start things off with this test during the Skype interview. Do this so programmers don't get surprised after they have provided a quote. Sometimes they're happy to get this test done without a charge but sometimes they want a small fee. In either case, be clear with this requirement and have them include it in the quote.

If you have selected your programmer and you're happy with the results of your initial test, you'll be well on your way to creating your first app. But if you're not happy with the results, don't hesitate to move on.

The process of finding programmers might take some time but this is time well spent. Don't cut any corners. This will help you avoid unnecessary delays, costs, and frustration in the future. You'll always be looking to add new talent to your team, so learning how to quickly and effectively assess programmers is an important skill to have.

HOW TO MANAGE PROGRAMMERS

It can take a lot of energy to find good programmers. The trick is to manage them properly on a daily basis to keep them happy and your business strong. These are some lessons I've learned along the way when it comes to managing programmers.

Stay on Top of What's Happening with Your Project

At some point, you might decide to hire programmers for full-time work. Until then, you will be working with companies and independent programmers who will have multiple projects running at the same time. This can lead to less than an optimal flow of information between you and programmers. They may not be as focused as they need to be with keeping you appraised of their progress. If left unchecked, this can lead to projects taking longer than they should and to a final product different from what you had in mind. You're the project manager and business owner, and it's your task to keep things on track rather than expecting the programmer to do this for you.

This is something I handled poorly early on. I was letting my developers take their time and didn't diligently check on progress. I learned to ask for milestones and timelines during the quoting process. This has allowed me to know how the app will look and function at each milestone and how long the project will take before a single line of code has been written. I periodically check in and review what's working and what still needs to be tweaked. We go back and forth like that from start to finish. Most applications go through multiple iterations during design and development, and I don't release partial payments until I'm fully satisfied with each milestone. Don't let your plane get off course for too long otherwise you could end up in Antarctica freezing your butt off.

Hire Slowly, Fire Quickly

Once you get a few apps under your belt, and things seem to be smooth with your developer or development team, you might want to consider hiring one of them for full-time work. While the flexibility of using subcontractors as needed is great, the danger is other clients can hire them and book them solid for months.

As soon as you feel you are happy with the work of particular programmers and are making some money, lock them in. I have several guys I keep on monthly retainers. They know I am going to spend a minimum amount of dollars every month with them, and as a return, they prioritize my projects.

If you notice problems, such as lack of responsiveness or sloppy work, cut your losses quickly and fire them. If you do not, they can become a drag on your company. Like with any breakup, you should part ways amicably. It's just business, and you don't want to piss people off who handle your assets.

The best way to fire programmers is to clarify they did not meet your expectations and you want to stop work. Salvage as much of the work as possible and compensate the programmer fairly, but move on as quickly as possible and chalk it up as learning a lesson.

HOW TO TEST YOUR APPS

Congratulations. You've gone through all of the development milestones, and you've got your app back. Before you pass out the champagne glasses, you need to do a few critical things. If you were having a house built, before you signed off, you'd want everything in working order. You would check major things like the roof and plumbing all the way down to minor things like the crown molding or anything cosmetic. You need to do the same thing with your app.

To start, the app must perform as expected. Pull out your initial design document and go through every feature. Never assume that something works because it worked last time you tested the app. Test each feature every time, especially before the final release. Don't stop here because, as the creator of your own app, you know how everything should work. It makes sense to you, but it might not to others.

If you worked for a major software development company, you would have a team of well-paid engineers to poke, prod, twist, and stretch your app any which way they could. As a solo, bootstrap appreneur, you probably don't have those resources. You can, however, accomplish the same thing with a resource that all of us have: our friends and family plan. Your job is to get everyone you know, from your 75-year-old grandmother to your 12-year-old nephew to test your app.

The time you spend on testing is crucial because you will see how consumers use your product, what's easy, what they don't understand, and their patterns. They will have questions that won't occur to you because you designed the app and everything about it is obvious to you.

Hand the app to them and say something like, "Hey check this out." Don't mention that it's your app, what it's supposed to do, or how it works. Give as little information as possible and watch them as they understand and navigate your app. This experience will be similar to the one your real user will have because you're not there to explain things to them as well. Watch them testing your app and ask yourself these questions:

1. Are they confused?
2. Are they stuck?

3. Are they complaining?
4. Are they using the app the way you intended?
5. Did they find a mistake (also called a bug) because of using the app in a different way?
6. Are they having fun?
7. Are they making suggestions for improvements? If yes, which ones?

Get them to tell about their experience with it. They will be more honest if they don't know the app is yours. Don't get offended if you hear something you don't like. This feedback is priceless. Assess each response to see if your app has a problem. Ask yourself these questions:

1. Would other users have the same issues? If yes, how can you fix it?
2. Should you move things around?
3. Should you change colors to improve visibility?
4. Would adding some instructions help?
5. Should you improve navigation?

I showed one of my latest apps to my friend, Jason. While he was testing it, he had a small problem. "Chad, it looks nice, and it seems pretty cool," he said. "But how do I get back to the main menu?"

"Right there," I said. "Where?" he asked. And it dawned on me. The back button was the same color as the background, and it was small. It was not registering as a button in his mind, and I realized this would be an issue for others. Those extra 10 minutes showing him the app paid off.

After you gather the feedback, have your programmers make the fixes or changes. You want to guarantee the app works on different models of iPhones, iPod Touches, and maybe iPads. Apple continues to innovate and come out with new devices every year. The more of these your app can support the better. This is something to discuss early on with your programmers. Make sure they create the app with the different devices in mind.

Again, you want to test your app on all these devices but that's impractical when you're getting started. It will be your programmers' job initially to test the app on all the different devices. I ask my programmers to create a detailed feature checklist that I look over and improve if necessary. I test each feature until everything works as expected.

Testing and debugging will take several iterations, like the design and development stages. This is all part of the process. Use the TestFlight app and service mentioned before to save lots of time with the mechanics of installing test versions of your app. At some point, you'll be wrapping up changes and sending the app off to the iTunes store for distribution.

It's a good idea to have your programmers show you or someone on your team how to submit your first few apps. Don't give out your online developer portal login information to your programmer or anybody else. The best way to do this is to use Skype or GoToMeeting and share your screen while they walk you through the process. As your business grows, you might want to delegate this work to someone on your team.

And keep in mind, all of this is much easier than it sounds. Now that you understand the importance and process of creating a development team, it's time to take things up a notch and have some fun. In the next chapter, we're going to discuss your most important job, which is marketing your apps.

What I Learned

1.
2.
3.

Actions to Take

1. Look for programmers.
2. Interview at least 10 and select the best three.
3. Create a thorough design for your app idea.
4. Get quotes from the three programmers you selected.
5. Choose one and test him.

6

Sex App-eal

Marketing Basics to Attract More Buyers

Any man has a chance to sweep any woman off her feet. He just needs the right broom.

—Hitch

"Get a hold of yourself, Chad. Not cool. Come on, man, get it together."

My mind raced as I walked awkwardly through the noisy crowd. I was a freshman in college, attending the first party of the year for the 2003 class. Colored lights dotted the room, songs by Snoop Dog, and Jay-Z blasted overhead, while kegs of beer were flowing like Niagara Falls.

The girls were wearing dresses and heels, and the guys looked as though they had walked out of a *GQ* magazine. I seemed to be the only one there who didn't get the memo about the dress code. Though everyone else was dressed for a night on the town, I was wearing a T-shirt, jeans, and sandals with socks. My hair was disheveled and my untrimmed beard made me appear as if I had walked in from a campsite rather than a magazine spread.

People were laughing and joking with each other. As I shuffled through the crowd, I tried to look confident. I threw out a smile, which somehow stayed stuck like I had been injected with Botox. I felt uncomfortable, self-conscious, and out of place.

As I walked through the crowd, I could feel the eyes of the people I walked past staring at me. I nervously jetted to the nearest open spot and sat down.

Suddenly, the most gorgeous girl I had ever seen walked by.

She had luscious long brown hair, deep ocean-blue eyes, and a smile that could light up a small city. She was wearing a classy, long, black dress that perfectly fit her tall, athletic body. Excitement and anxiety swept over my body like a tsunami, reckless and uncontrollable.

I felt compelled to stand up, walk to her, and say something.

"Hi, uh," I stammered. "This is a cool place."

"Yeah, it is," she said as she sized me up by glancing at my evening attire. I could tell she had made up her mind. I had lost her at hello and since I had used all my oxygen on those five words, I had nothing left to say. I gave her a nervous smile and turned away. She disappeared.

I felt like a complete loser, empty and rejected. I realized I didn't know the first thing about making myself attractive to the opposite sex. It didn't matter who I was or what I had to offer because the outside wrapping didn't match what was inside.

In other words, I was clueless how to market myself. I was sure I had a great product, but I didn't know how to package it. I didn't know how to attract interest.

After a while, I decided to leave the party. As I was making my way to the door, I heard laughter coming from another room. I looked to see what was going on.

A group of beautiful women were intently listening to one guy telling a funny story. He was dressed in a sports coat and designer jeans that said "expensive." His hair was perfect, and his posture commanded attention. Every move he made exuded confidence.

He must have been saying all the right things because the girls were laughing, and I saw more people gathering around, leaning in to hear what he was saying.

How did he do it?

I knew the answer to my question. People were drawn to him because he looked great and said the right things. He was confident and owned the room. His name was Monaco.

As I made my way home, I decided I would learn from him, so I could light up a room when I walked in. I befriended Monaco, who later taught me how he was able to draw people in and entertain them. After that, my social life changed.

I was still the same guy who had cluelessly walked into that first party, but I had learned how to present myself to get a new result. The lesson translated well in business. At a fundamental level, that's how all marketing works. You want to create an experience that intrigues people from the beginning, so they feel confident with their decision to invest their time.

The app stores are filled with thousands of great apps, but most developers are not skilled enough in marketing. Meanwhile, many poorly designed apps rank highly because their developers have figured out the marketing game.

To be successful in the app business, you don't need to come up with the most innovative app on the planet. All you need to do is provide value and understand the strategies to market your apps so your customers discover and purchase them.

In this chapter, I show you simple but powerful marketing techniques that will drive traffic and get customers flocking to your apps.

DRESSED TO KILL

As with any business, you will have to set yourself apart from the competition. Your app needs to be a well-designed, quality app, but the best app in the world won't do you much good if people can't find it or, when they do find it, they are unconvinced of its value and choose not to download it.

Most developers focus almost exclusively on creating apps and severely underestimate the importance of implementing some of the most basic marketing techniques. These techniques are effective and won't cost much. You should consider them part of the app development process. As you grow your business, you can spend some money on more advanced marketing. (I discuss this in Chapter 8.) I recommend you don't do this until you have seen demand for your app and have started to make money with it.

Here's the formula for app success:

$$\text{Effective marketing} = \text{Traffic} = \text{Downloads} = \$\$\$ = \text{Happy Business Owner}$$

This is a no brainer, but most people don't pay attention to it. The more effective your marketing, the more people will see your apps. The more people see your apps, the more downloads and dollars you will get. Think of it as a numbers game. For instance, assume that you have 10,000 people looking at your app every day and you converted only 1 percent of them. That would give you 100 downloads a day and for a paid app that's $70 a day which is about $2,100 a month. That's one app with a rather low conversion rate. So, remember that your job is to create great apps and to put in the same time and effort to get them in front of as many eye balls as possible. Sure, you're going to get some visibility by being in Apple's App Store, but with so many apps there, you can't count on that.

So, how do you dress up an app?

During the impulse buy discussion in Chapter 3, we learned that users typically assess the icon, title, description, and screenshots before downloading an app. Understanding how each of these basic elements of an app are marketing opportunities that allow you to dress up your app is essential to being successful in the app business. Your job is to create a seamless flow from the icon all the way to the download button. Let's take a closer look at each one of these.

ICONS

The icon is the first thing users will see when they are checking out your apps. It's the small square image with the rounded corners to the left of the app title. It's also the image that users see on their phone after they install your app.

The icon is important because it's how the users will identify with your app. It should capture the essence of the app. It must look good, attract the users' attention, and compel them to investigate your app. It's the visual ID of your app.

The icon is the first impression you will make on the users. The old expression "you don't get a second chance to make a first impression" applies here. Would you want to show up in your pajamas or your best suit to a job interview? Make sure you have a quality icon that represents your app and makes the users feel it has value.

Your icon should appeal to the customers you want to attract. If the icon displays a cute, cartoon animal, you probably won't look in it for help with navigation, right? Many developers create icons as an afterthought and focus all of their effort on the app itself. It's crucial to work with your programmers and graphic designers during the design phase of your project to craft the icon for your app.

APP TITLE

Your title should be exciting, snappy, trendy, and catchy. If it meets these criteria, people naturally are going to want to check it out. But the title of your app is more than just a name. (See Figure 6.1.) It is also critical in helping users find your app when they perform a keyword search on the app store. Each word in your title serves as the most valuable keyword, much like keywords in search engines. Think of the title as your URL. If you type "angry" into the App Store search field, the Angry Birds apps will return as a search result.

Your title needs to be memorable and specific to what your app does. When deciding on a title for your app, consider other successful apps in the App Store. I do this often, and ask myself the following three questions:

1. Why are these titles working?
2. What makes these catchy?
3. What terms are people searching for to find these apps?

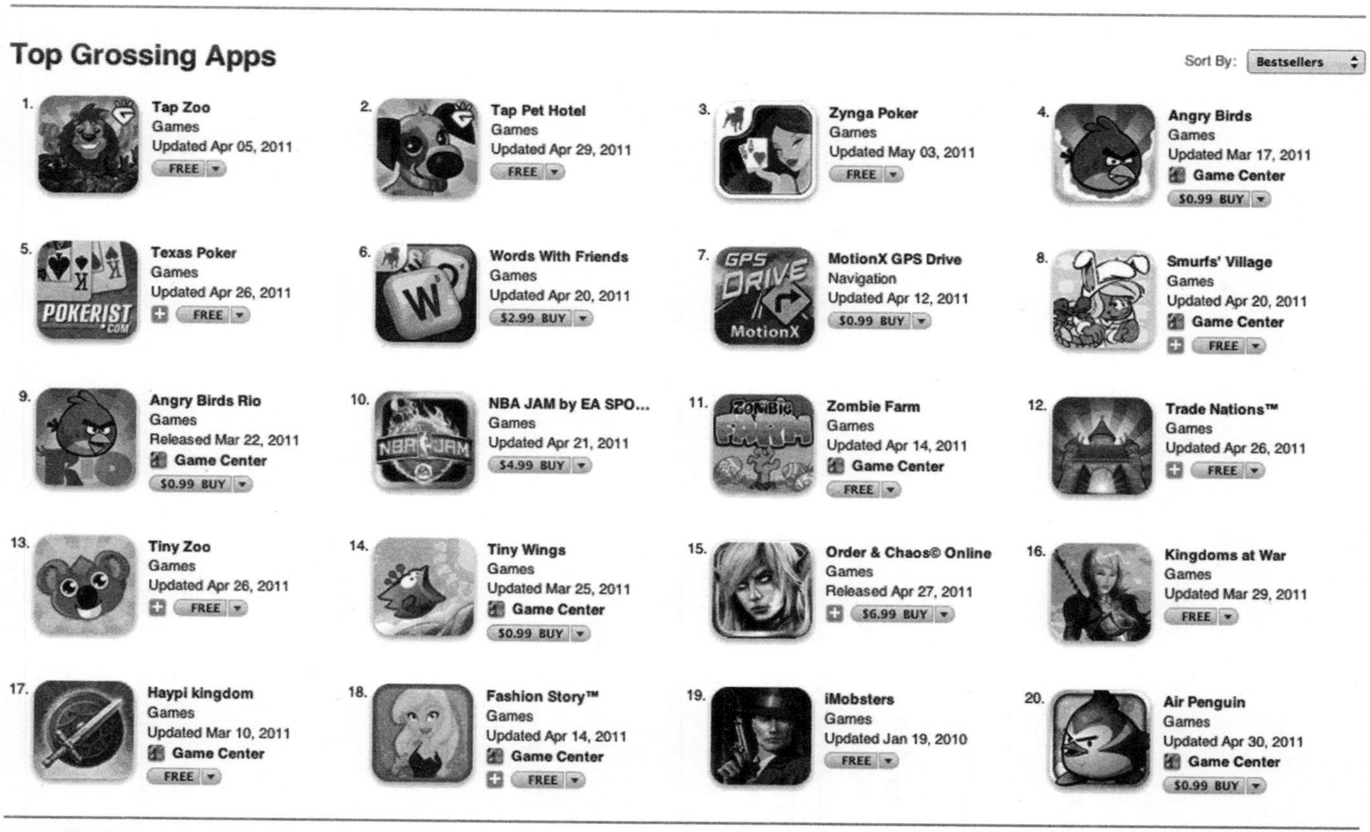
Top Grossing Apps
Sort By: Bestsellers
1. Tap Zoo
Games
Updated Apr 05, 2011
FREE
2. Tap Pet Hotel
Games
Updated Apr 29, 2011
FREE
3. Zynga Poker
Games
Updated May 03, 2011
FREE
4. Angry Birds
Games
Updated Mar 17, 2011
Game Center
$0.99 BUY
5. Texas Poker
Games
Updated Apr 26, 2011
FREE
POKERIST.COM
6. Words With Friends
Games
Updated Apr 20, 2011
$2.99 BUY
7. MotionX GPS Drive
Navigation
Updated Apr 12, 2011
$0.99 BUY
GPS DRIVE
MotionX
8. Smurfs' Village
Games
Updated Apr 20, 2011
Game Center
FREE
9. Angry Birds Rio
Games
Released Mar 22, 2011
Game Center
$0.99 BUY
10. NBA JAM by EA SPO...
Games
Updated Apr 21, 2011
$4.99 BUY
NBA JAM
11. Zombie Farm
Games
Updated Apr 14, 2011
Game Center
FREE
12. Trade Nations™
Games
Updated Apr 26, 2011
FREE
13. Tiny Zoo
Games
Updated Apr 26, 2011
FREE
14. Tiny Wings
Games
Updated Mar 25, 2011
Game Center
$0.99 BUY
15. Order & Chaos© Online
Games
Released Apr 27, 2011
$6.99 BUY
16. Kingdoms at War
Games
Updated Mar 29, 2011
FREE
17. Haypi kingdom
Games
Updated Mar 10, 2011
Game Center
FREE
18. Fashion Story™
Games
Updated Apr 14, 2011
Game Center
FREE
19. iMobsters
Games
Updated Jan 19, 2010
FREE
20. Air Penguin
Games
Updated Apr 30, 2011
Game Center
$0.99 BUY

FIGURE 6.1 Top grossing app titles.

It helps to think about words in your title as the vehicles of users who will find your app. It's fun to create cute names, but it's not so much fun if nobody can find them.

When naming your apps, keep in mind the Chomp analytics (mentioned in Chapter 3). Over 90 percent of searches in the App Store are focused on the functionality of the app rather than a specific app name. So, when you're deciding whether to name your app Fun Colors or Flashlight you should go with the more descriptive name, which is Flashlight.

DESCRIPTIONS

Next comes the description. Having a compelling description for your app is like having a great opening line. People are more willing to learn more about you if you pique their interest. Following the impulse buy theory, you should not have an overly long description. Most people won't take the time to read the whole thing.

The first chunk of the description needs to be packed with information. It should tell users just about everything they need to know about the app. You should make it interesting or funny. Add two or three sentences of marketing copy here. Where applicable, use statements like "Top App 2012" or "One of the Most Addictive Games in the App Store." Then, follow it up with a call to action such as, "Check out the screenshots and see for yourself."

For example, the description for Fingerprint Security (Figure 6.2) starts with the short headline:

One of the Top Apps Worldwide

This marketing copy would not apply to all apps. If you're starting out, you can write other descriptions that catch users' attention by pointing out how your app is different and better than the competition and by including testimonials. For instance, if I were starting out with Fingerprint Security, I would write something like this: "The Most Realistic Fingerprint Scanner Prank in the App Store." Or get a positive testimonial from a user, such as, "This app blew my mind. Its sounds and graphics are unbelievable." Another example is "Free for a limited time."

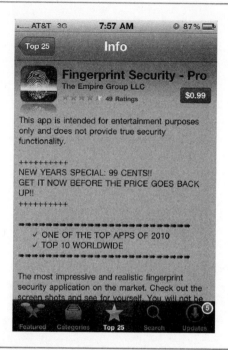

FIGURE 6.2   Fingerprint Security - Pro description.

This gives customers a sense of urgency and incentive to download the app.

After this description, follow it with a few sentences explaining why the users must download this app: "The most impressive and realistic fingerprint security application on the market. Check out the screenshots and see for yourself. You will not be disappointed."

SCREENSHOTS

Screenshots are pictures you supply with your app description to show the customer your app. Consider them the graphical description of your app. The trailer to the movie, so to speak. Basic screenshots are images that are screen captures of the app. More advanced screenshots are graphic designs that are appealing, contain marketing, and convey how the app works (see Figure 6.3).

Screenshots are great marketing tools because they give a snapshot of what users will experience using your app. Many people shopping

iPhone Screenshots

FIGURE 6.3 Basic screenshot (top); Advanced screenshop (bottom).

for apps often don't read the description but instead scroll down to the screenshots. The screenshots need to convey the main functionality of the app without showing too many details that may confuse users. If your screenshots are cluttered, it will be as ineffective as selling a house with messy rooms. The brain gets overwhelmed and buyers have more trouble seeing the product's true value. Therefore, the screenshots you include should be clean, appealing, and informative so users are not overwhelmed yet are compelled to download the app.

When I started out, I used screen captures of my apps to create basic screenshots. The capture was simple; most developers were doing this. While looking through the app store, I noticed some successful apps had more elaborate screenshots. They were adding banners that attracted the user's attention and explained the benefits of the app. I tried these advanced screenshots for one of my apps and the results convinced me to create them for all of my apps.

These days almost all top apps have advanced screenshots. Most developers have understood that their screenshots are a major tool to make an impression on users. This is another reason why you must work with a team that has a graphic designer. Your graphics guy will create the graphics in your app and your icon and will create killer screenshots that persuade the users to buy the app now.

Also, be aware that the sequence of your screenshots is important. You can showcase a maximum of five images. Be sure your screenshots tell a story that compels users to click the download button (see Figure 6.4).

These are great examples of advanced graphics. Through the images, users quickly understand how the app works. Text banners further clarify each step, and as an added bonus, these advanced screenshots include the app's graphics.

KEYWORDS

Unlike your icon and title, keywords are not something the users get to see. When you submit your app on the App Store, you're allowed to provide keywords relevant to your app. When users search for one of the terms you chose, your app appears in the search results.

For example, if you type in the word "kids" or "game" on the App Store, you will find that Angry Birds is one of the search results. The terms "kids" and "game" are not in the app title, therefore, the makers of Angry Birds most likely chose those keywords to associate with their app. This makes perfect sense as Angry Birds appeals to a lot of kids and anybody searching with those terms will find the app.

As you can see, keywords are important because your target demographic will use them to find your apps. Each word in your app title

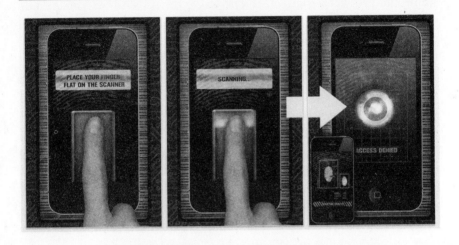

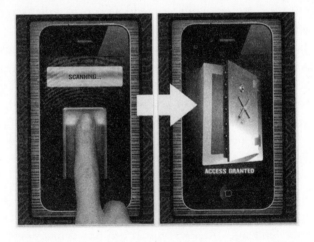

FIGURE 6.4 Screenshots that tell a story.

represents a keyword, so you don't have to repeat them when you're providing the keywords during app submission.

The best way to determine keywords for your app is to think like users. What is your target audience searching for? Do not use keywords that are irrelevant because you can only provide a limited amount of keywords. When Apple introduced the keyword tool some time after the App Store opened, I added keywords I thought people would be searching for. For my app, Fingerprint Security, I used terms like "camera" and "video." I thought that's how the keyword tool worked and my rationale was that if people were searching for a camera app, they might see my app and get interested in it.

I realized that app shopping is like any other kind of shopping. If you go in for batteries and walk past a toothbrush, you're not likely to buy a toothbrush when all you need are batteries. So, the keywords must be relevant, or users will ignore your product even if it's part of the search results.

A good example of effective keyword usage is an app I created called Flashlight. Since the name is Flashlight, we came up with keywords, such as "bright," "help," "light," and "camping."

When coming up with keywords, consider these three questions:

1. What is the demographic?
2. What are the users' needs?
3. What are they searching for?

I don't use any particular tools to brainstorm for keywords. I use common sense and think like an app user.

CATEGORIES

Most app stores organize apps into specific categories to help users find them more easily. Some of the categories in the App Store include Games, Entertainment, Utilities, Books, Business, Education, and so on. In addition to the top overall rankings of all apps, each category has its own top rankings and, therefore, generates a certain amount of visibility based on these charts. An app that doesn't show up in the top 200 overall, might still be in the top 10 of a particular category. Users looking for certain apps often browse through these category charts without looking at the top overall charts.

When you're submitting your app for review, you have to select the category you would like your app to appear in. Make sure to select the most relevant category for your app. For example, an alarm clock app should be in the Utilities category rather than in the Games category. On the other hand, many apps could be classified into more than one category. You have to choose one but you can change the category during an update. Some categories are more competitive than others. Check out the categories of competing apps to see which category they seem to be popular in. This is usually a good indication of where you should place your app.

THE POWER OF FREE APPS

Prepare the basic marketing elements mentioned above for all of your apps. After you take care of the basics, your greatest marketing tool will be free apps. They generate traffic and visibility that you otherwise wouldn't get. Using free apps is the equivalent of having a brick and mortar retail business on Main Street as opposed to five miles outside of town.

Free apps create the most traffic because they have the smallest barrier to entry. It takes five seconds to download, and it's free. Why wouldn't you push the button? More free apps are downloaded than paid apps. After all, if you can't give away your app for free, how are you going to get people to pay for it? Once the free version of your app gains some traction, you can use it to advertise the paid version of the same app. This is like getting those free food samples at the supermarket. If you like the sample you tasted, you might go buy the whole bag and become a long-term customer.

In Chapter 9, I show you how to take that free traffic and convert it into dollars. Using the free apps as part of your marketing strategy will dramatically increase the likelihood of having a successful paid app.

COURSE CORRECTING

After you launch the free version of your app, you need to give it some time to generate interest. I give it about one to two weeks while I assess the incoming data and continue the market research. During that time, the App Store customers will vote with their downloads, and let you know whether your idea or marketing is working.

Give the marketing basics your best shot for your app launch, but you will not always hit the bull's-eye with your first attempt. You must understand and accept this concept. Most developers make the mistake of ignoring these marketing basics. Of those developers who don't make this mistake, many make another mistake, which is to think that they need to worry about the marketing only once. They create an icon they like, pick a title that excites them, and publish the app.

When it doesn't work out, they blame the app. "It was just not a good app" or "The market was not ready for it" are some of the excuses. This may be true, but their initial marketing angle may not have been the correct one even though the app was good.

Just as your app will always need certain refinements due to consumer demand and competition, so will your marketing. What makes an app successful is improving it and making regular adjustments or additions to all its marketing elements. For most of my apps, I have changed the icon and screenshots three to five times and the title and description between 5 and 10 times. I change keywords almost every time I update apps. I always switch the categories when it makes sense. Keep an open mind and continue to be inspired by your observations during your market research.

For example, one time, I added the term "phone" to the keywords of my free prank fingerprint app. This seemingly minor change propelled the app to the number one top overall free category. It was advertising the pro version at the same time, so this shot the pro version to number 27 top overall paid and had a major effect on some of the other apps since I was cross-promoting everything. This one change moved the income of the company from around $1,000 a day to about $3,000 a day. This is the power of tweaking your app marketing. One change can dramatically increase your revenue.

When making these changes, keep your speed of implementation in mind. Whatever you want to do, you must do quickly. You have to have a team in place to make marketing tweaks because if you want to change a screenshot and it takes a month to do it, you'll possibly miss out on the benefit of that change. This equates to leaving a certain amount of money on the table. Also, do not change too many things at one time because then you won't be able to track what's working. Do not mess too much with apps that are doing well since you don't want to reverse your success.

Once your customers purchase the app, the marketing doesn't stop there though. You have to wow them and turn them into raving fans, so they'll spread the word about your app and come back for more. You have to give them reasons to keep coming back to your app. These reasons may include improved functionality, new options, or new levels. If your customers have a positive experience with one app, they will likely buy more apps or upgrades.

How do you know if your marketing is working? Analytics. They show you everything you need to know about what's happening in your app. It's crucial to the health of your business. So, follow along in the next chapter.

What I Learned

1.
2.
3.

Actions to Take

1. For each one of your new and existing apps, research the App Store for icons, titles, keywords, categories, descriptions, and screenshots of successful competitor apps.
2. Create free apps as part of your marketing strategy.
3. Systematically tweak your app marketing.

7

Keeping Score

What to Measure to Win the App Game

Sometimes we think we're losing the game of life when we're really winning simply because we're not keeping score.

—Anthony Robbins

I stepped off the train and onto the platform in Berkeley, California, and was met with a blast of hot, dense air. It was an unseasonably warm day, and without question I was wearing the wrong outfit. I had relocated to San Francisco in hopes of learning more about the mobile app space and growing my business. I didn't know anyone, and I felt a bit uncertain in this new city and in my business.

I was on my way to meet a top apprenuer who had randomly emailed me the previous week in the hopes of networking. I wanted to make a good first impression, so I had to project confidence in this arena even though I had been in this business for only a few months.

Alan was pleasant. We met at his favorite lunch joint, the infamous Smokehouse. While clogging our arteries with what he called the best burgers and hot dogs in America, we began to discuss the app business.

"How many downloads do you have per day?" Alan asked.

Not knowing the answer, but wanting to appear informed, I estimated, "Umm, we are doing about one to two K a day."

"Cool. And you have free apps with traffic pointing to your paid apps, I'm assuming?" he continued.

"Uh, yeah. We are working on that right now," I deflected.

Dodging more questions, I asked, "How is business going for you?" *Phew,* I thought, I'd be able to avoid more questions by getting him to discuss what he did, but he was just getting started. He continued with his relentless barrage of questions:

"How many active users do you have?"

"How many banner ad clicks do you have inside your apps?"

"Do you have a nag screen?"

"Is it converting?"

"You have a 'More' button, right?"

"Are you translating your marketing materials into other languages?"

After this onslaught of questions and my vague and uncertain responses, he and I knew how clueless I was with my own business.

I just wanted to scream, "I don't know!!!"

But, why didn't I know?

As soon as I asked myself that question, a light bulb went off, along with a hallelujah, followed by an open hand slap to the back of the head, with a Homer Simpson-like "D'oh!" I had been unknowingly neglecting one of the most critical elements of my business. Could that be why I was not achieving the goals I had set for my business?

I was focused and was able to develop new apps quickly, but I wasn't following through on what I was creating. I wasn't tracking my results and strategically improving my apps based on that data. That one seemingly minor distinction to measure *everything* was a complete game changer and allowed me to take my business to a new level. I could make informed decisions and adjustments on the fly and have measurable results.

Tracking your app stats gives you more clarity and control over your business. Without solid data, all you have are limited perceptions about what is going on. You must scrutinize the metrics of each app you create and understand what you can do to maximize visibility, downloads, and user activity. When you understand these trends, you can dissect the info and start diagnosing and testing ways to improve your overall revenue.

It's like going to the doctor when you feel something might be off. Initially, the doctor doesn't know the problem, so he or she asks you questions and tests you to measure your condition. Once the doctor has a conclusion based on the data, he or she can prescribe a treatment to see if it fixes things. If that doesn't work, the doctor moves to the next feasible treatment until you're healthy again.

In this chapter, I show you what to look for in your data. You'll understand what stats to check, what tracking software to use, and how to use the data to tweak your apps, boost traffic, and earn more money.

THE STATS THAT MATTER

I have found that the most important stats to track for your app business are your traffic, rankings, user activity, and revenue.

Traffic

Most developers look at the number of downloads their apps are generating because they want to know how much money they have made. This makes sense and is important, but you must look at app downloads as your traffic. The more free and paid downloads your have, the more traffic you are generating.

This traffic can be used in many ways to further monetize your apps. It's almost as if each one of your apps is acting like a website that attracts a certain number of visitors daily. That visibility is of tremendous value when directed properly. I examine the daily downloads of every one of my apps. If I see the number slipping, I try to understand why and take immediate action to bring back the traffic.

Rankings

As mentioned in Chapter 3, the App Store constantly shows the popularity of apps based on the number of downloads and other undisclosed metrics. As talked about previously, Apple has top overall app charts and category-specific ones. Your apps must appear in these lists because of the additional visibility they provide. Your app's position in these lists can be considered its ranking. (See Figure 7.1.)

Tracking app rankings is something that most developers neglect because they think they have no control over it. That couldn't be further from the truth. Your rankings are an important metric when it comes to assessing your app's performance, and you can improve your rankings through various marketing techniques. I'm constantly focused on getting my apps ranked, and once they are in the charts, I keep close tabs on their rankings. If I see an app slipping in the charts, I immediately focus on it and figure out why that's happening and what can be done to raise the ranking.

User Activity

Yes, it's great for users to download your apps, but your ultimate outcome is to turn them into customers who use your app consistently. Every user interaction presents an opportunity to monetize your app portfolio. The only way to know if your users are loving your apps is to track the user activity within your app. The nice thing is that it's easy with Flurry. You can track anything, such as how many times a button is being touched or how often the app is used.

For example, at one point I saw in the reviews of one of my apps that the users didn't even know how to use the app. Needless to say they

FIGURE 7.1   Top paid apps rankings.

weren't happy. This was surprising to me because the app had an instructions page. Perplexed, I decided to track how many people were clicking the button to open the instructions, and to my surprise only five percent of users were opening them. To fix this problem, I made the button more visible and after that small tweak, 70 percent of users were clicking the instructions button. From that point on, more people left positive reviews and my app became more successful.

Revenue

All of the previous metrics are indicators for the most important and obvious metric: your revenue. You have to track your revenue every day and continuously observe your daily, monthly, and quarterly trends.

This sounds obvious, but it's easy to overlook revenue as a metric that can be tuned like the others. As soon as I see any positive or negative change in revenue, I want to understand what's causing that activity. Do my apps have more or less traffic? Did they move up or down in rankings? Has user activity increased or decreased? I want to understand what is causing the change in revenue and take action accordingly. Every change in revenue is an opportunity to understand the intricacies of your app business. Again, this might sound tedious, but it's very simple to do. App sales will not be your only source of revenue. You will make money from banner ads and affiliate marketing, so check on all sources of revenue daily to get the complete picture.

TOOLS FOR TRACKING STATS

You have various ways to monitor your app metrics. One option is Apple's Developer Portal. Apple shows you the number of downloads, your revenue, when you will be paid, and even your iAd banner advertising statistics. The site is intuitive and useful. (See Figure 7.2.)

Even though this is nice, I prefer AppFigures (appempire.com/app figures). AppFigures is great for tracking numbers as well as other aspects

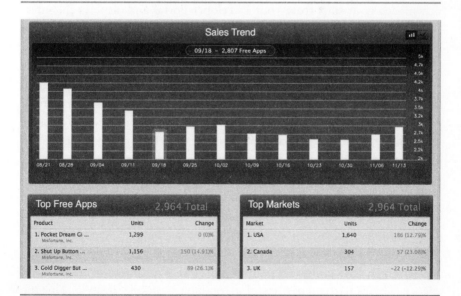

FIGURE 7.2   Apple developer portal stats.

FIGURE 7.3   AppFigures.

of your business. (See Figure 7.3.) Once set up, the site automatically downloads your stats from your Developer Portal and displays the information in a much more intuitive way. You can investigate one app at a time or all of your apps together. You can see your app rankings and reviews. You can review your app downloads over time or based on countries.

AppFigures sends daily e-mails that summarize the previous day's app stats. This is nice because you don't have to log in to get the information. I receive an e-mail every morning that gives me a breakdown of apps by the number of downloads and the amount of net profit (see Figure 7.4). Plus, I get a breakdown of the iAd profits. This is convenient and is like getting a daily check-up for your business.

App Annie is another service similar to AppFigures (appempire.com/appannie). Like AppFigures, App Annie shows your apps' movement and rankings and how much money you're making. App Annie also shows you the historical ranking data of all apps in the App Store.

There are also mobile apps that can give you this information at a glance. This is particularly useful if you have a mobile lifestyle. The app I use is Position App (Figure 7.5), which shows your apps' rankings and whether other apps are moving up or down in popularity.

FIGURE 7.4   Daily AppFigures summary e-mail.

Also a useful tool for tracking user activity within your apps is Flurry (appempire.com/flurry). This takes bit of extra programming within your apps but can give you powerful insights, such as how often and for what duration your customers are using your apps.

USING STATS TO YOUR ADVANTAGE

We talked about the importance of constantly improving your app marketing in Chapter 6. It's not only about how good your apps are. It's about how good you are at quickly and appropriately adjusting to market changes. Constant improvement is the mechanism that moves this business forward and keeps it sustainable.

FIGURE 7.5   PositionApp ranking trends.

How do you know what to improve? Stats. You can make changes based on your hunches and see if something hits, or you can take full advantage of the data you'll be getting to make informed decisions.

These are the questions you need to ask yourself while reviewing your stats and thinking about how to improve your apps:

- Has the app gone up or down in the rankings? Why?
- Are there more or fewer downloads and in what countries? Why?
- Could I be doing more to promote and market my app?
- Is my marketing converting, or do I need to do a better job?
- What do the reviews say? Can I fix the things people are complaining about? (I don't recommend following everybody's advice, but if you discover a negative trend, fix it.)

- Do people like this app? How often do they use it?
- How can I add more value for my users?
- Can I monetize this app better? How?

Icon:

- Is there a style of icon for a competing app that I can emulate?
- Can I keep my current design but try different colors?
- Are users able to understand what the app is for by looking at the icon?
- Am I sticking to icons similar to the ones that have proven themselves in the market, or am I trying to be overly creative?

Title:

- Is my title clear?
- Does my title describe the app's functionality?
- Does my title use strong keywords?

Description:

- How can I make my description less cluttered and easier to read?
- How can I better explain the functionality of my app?
- How can I make it more exciting?
- Do I have a call to action?

Screenshots:

- Can I make my screenshots more impressive visually?
- Do their themes fit the theme of the icon and rest of the app?
- How can I make my screenshots less cluttered and easier to understand?
- Do they have text banners that explain the functionality?
- Can I improve the text banners to mention more and better features?

Keywords:

- What words does my target demographic use to look for my app?
- What keywords are the competitors using?
- What other relevant keywords can I test?
- Am I using all the space available for keywords (100 characters)?

Categories:

- What other category could my app be in?
- What category are the competing apps in?
- What category is less competitive and might provide more visibility?

You have to be like a coach slicing through game footage. You need to review your game plan every day to decide what changes to make. Most developers take the shotgun approach and attack the problem by improving everything simultaneously. The worst part is if something works, they don't know what it was because they changed ten things at once. You must test each one of your changes individually so you can determine which changes are actually effective.

Improving an app's performance can be simple. One of my apps, Alarm Security, wasn't working, and I was trying to bring it back up in the rankings. I initially tried changing the name and keywords, and it didn't move much. The one thing I hadn't tried was switching it out of the Entertainment category. Since it was more of a utility app anyway, I decided to move it to the Utility category. The reason I had placed it in the Entertainment category was the app contained various alarm sounds, like loud screams or gunshots. I assumed users would use it more as a goof than as a tool, but I was wrong.

Once I moved the app into the utilities category, the number of downloads skyrocketed. After five days, the paid downloads nearly tripled, and it was only because of a category change. If I wasn't constantly working and improving the low performers, I could have easily missed this change that paid off in a big way.

One of the questions I often get is, "How long should I test a tweak?" When you tweak something to make it better, measure the results for about one week before you make other changes. You'll see quickly if your improvements are producing positive results.

Keep your budget in mind. A lot of these tweaks won't cost you any money like changing the title, keywords, description, and categories. You should try those first. You can make some changes to the icon and screenshots, but keep costs as low as possible. Do not dump thousands of dollars into your improvements while you're still testing the market demand for your app and trying to recoup your investment. Work on improving the app only after you have gained traction with your marketing tweaks.

I recommend you set up a specific time you check in with your stats on a daily basis. Set up a routine that works for you and stick to it. When you are reviewing your stats and asking yourself the questions above, you will have many ideas for improvement. Make sure that these don't get lost. Capture and implement them one by one. Keep track of your changes and follow up with them because otherwise you will be unable to learn which of your changes had a positive effect. You can check out appempire.com/trackchanges for a spreadsheet that will allow you to easily track your changes.

PAYING ATTENTION TO REVIEWS

Another good way to find what you need to improve in your apps are your app reviews. The App Store allows people who have downloaded your app to rate it (one to five stars) and leave a brief text review. (See Figure 7.6.) You will get more reviews as your apps gain popularity. Some of them will be great, some not so much. Cue violin and tissues.

FIGURE 7.6   Reviews of Angry Birds.

It's crucial to view user reviews as constructive criticism. They may show you that you have a bug in your app you don't know about or reveal certain features that a lot of users would like to see.

Launching the Tic Tac Toe app was another great lesson for me about the importance of reviews. In its first version, the app flashed a sign when people won a game. But multiple reviews mentioned that there were no sounds, and that they wanted to be able to play against their friends. I used the customer feedback and had my developer add sounds and a multi-user feature. After that, one of the previous reviewers came back and said, "Hey, thanks for the change. These sounds are great." You could see it made that customers happy, and it was great marketing for the app.

As bad reviews can have a negative effect on your income, positive reviews can bolster sales. Reviews that are funny, exciting, and give credibility to your app will convert more customers. If the reviews are great, you may want to include them in your app description.

Something else you can do to get more feedback is to check your reviews from other parts of the world. It helps to get a perspective of how your apps are being received globally. You can use the AppFigures service to check what people in different counties are saying about your apps. AppFigures will translate the reviews for you. These translations are not perfect, but most of the time you will get the message. Priceless.

CUTTING YOUR LOSSES

Like most businesses, the app business is a numbers game. Some apps are going to work, and some aren't. Sometimes apps don't perform as expected even if you have an awesome icon, exciting screenshots, an appealing name, and a well-designed app. This is why I don't spend a lot of money to begin with until I see a demand in the market for the app. After you've tried to improve your app and its marketing elements based on the suggestions mentioned earlier in this chapter for three to four months, it's time to move on and focus your energy on a different app. Like any relationship or investment, cutting losses is difficult, but it's vital for you and your business.

For instance, I had created a paid app called Flashlight, which used the iPhone's camera flash to turn the phone into a flashlight. For about nine months, the app did alright. I noticed sales were falling. I focused on improving the core marketing components for a few months yet the app's sales still declined. At that point, I had to decide to cut my losses and stop investing time and money in the app. I decided to make Flashlight a free app and use it to funnel traffic to my other apps. Although Flashlight never became a huge money maker, it contributed to the overall ecosystem of my app business funneling traffic to my other apps.

Now that you understand the importance of measuring and how to tweak your apps, in the next chapter, you're going to learn how to increase your firepower with some advanced marketing techniques.

What I Learned

1.
2.
3.

Actions to Take

1. Sign up for AppFigures or App Annie and start becoming familiar with these tools.
2. Sign up for Flurry to track activity within your apps.
3. Decide what activity to track within your apps and why that information is important.
4. Set up a schedule to check in with the stats daily.
5. Create a simple spreadsheet to measure your changes.

8

Ninja Techniques that Will Grow Your Business

Advanced Marketing Tips and Tricks

Notice that the stiffest tree is most easily cracked, while the bamboo or willow survives by bending with the wind.

—Bruce Lee

Once I figured out that being able to market myself was essential, my confidence and ability to attract people soared. I felt as though I had discovered some type of superpower, and I was never going back. I went on a few dates and even ended up getting together with the beautiful blue-eyed girl, Vicky, whom I had struck out with at the freshman party. As we got to know each other, like at the start of any relationship, everything was new, exciting, and magical.

"I'm in love," I proclaimed to my college roommate Jeffrey, who smirked and rolled his eyes. Without a warning, a few months in, things began to change. As the relationship got more serious, there were expectations we each had that the other wasn't meeting. The honeymoon was over. I needed to understand more to keep the relationship alive and thriving.

"What do I do now?" I asked my friends. Through multiple conversations they made me realize that it takes a different set of skills and a deeper level of understanding to keep a relationship going and take it to the next level. They were right. What had worked in the beginning wasn't enough anymore and I had to step up my game.

A similar pattern can happen in business as well. Initially, everything seems great because you experience immediate and significant growth when you start from zero. You attract a great customer base with your initial marketing. You see your traffic and income grow, and you think your growth spurt will never end. At some point, you hit a wall, and you watch as your business starts to plateau or drop off. As with any business, you can't become complacent with your initial success and must be open to implementing new strategies to keep your business strong.

In the app world, many advanced marketing strategies are available to attract new users and keep them coming back, upgrading, and spending more money.

Every technique I talk about in this chapter is designed to drive as much traffic as possible to your apps and keep them from stagnating. The beauty of these techniques is that most of them are free and don't necessarily require more time or effort. By using a few of these advanced tactics, you can catapult yourself from app newbie to app expert.

HITTING A PLATEAU

I knew the after party had ended for my first app as soon as I saw the numbers dropping for a week straight. I realized I had gotten complacent and had stopped experimenting with new marketing strategies because I had been making good money.

Taking the hint, I sprang into action but continued to see my numbers decline for about a month and a half. I tried strategies that had worked previously but to no avail. I watched, trying new things, as revenue dropped from more than $900 a day to about $300 a day. I was not about to give up and began testing a bunch of new strategies to generate more revenue. Every week, I would use a new marketing technique to see if I could invigorate my fading app.

Finally, after some trial and error, a few of these techniques worked, and the downtrend reversed. Two months later, I was consistently averaging more than $800 a day. I was back in the game and those skills I learned were priceless.

These tested advanced techniques include the app network, nag screens, more pages, push notifications, the developer network, updates, and paid traffic.

YOUR APP NETWORK

I like the phrase "no man is an island." It means that human beings can't thrive when isolated from others. This is true for apps as well. You can create a single app that may do well, but when you create additional apps and link them to each other with cross-promotion, you'll move toward your app empire's full financial potential.

An app network is a web of interconnected apps that use their active users (traffic) to promote each other. As mentioned in Chapter 7, you should consider each one of your apps as a source of traffic much like a website on the Internet. This traffic contains gold, especially if you use the power of your app network to monetize it.

For example, if you only have one free app that is doing 50,000 downloads a day, you will be making a certain amount of money with banner advertising and perhaps some affiliate marketing. If you have multiple apps that promote each other with nag screens and promo pages (which will be explained), then you can funnel those 50,000 users to your other apps and generate hundreds of additional dollars. That's essentially the app network: your own superhighway of app users that you direct and redirect on a consistent basis to find the traffic patterns that yield the most amount of money.

The app network is so vital that few if any app companies can be successful for a long period of time without building one. Your app network allows you to boost your app rankings and gives you credibility with other app developers, which makes them more likely to cross-promote with you. It's crucial when it comes to launching a new app because you can immediately get lots of eyeballs on it using your app network. The more downloads and traffic you get with your app network the more you start growing a vibrant app ecosystem. Most major players have figured this out, which is why they can push their apps into the top rankings consistently.

This is why you have to make developing your app network a priority from day one. You're in the business of creating apps and in the business of creating a kick-ass app network. Most of the following sections in this chapter will focus on teaching you how to do that.

NAG SCREENS

Have you ever been to a nice restaurant where the waitress upsells you? She says, "Hey, that pesto pasta is awesome. Would you like me to add some shrimp to that?" You think about it for a second and sometimes say, "Sure. Why not?" You didn't think about the shrimp, but when presented with the option, you went for it.

That's the job of the nag screen (see Figure 8.1). It's a pop-up window that appears when an app is started. It has a short call to action, giving the users the option to download the pro version of the app that has more features than the one they downloaded.

The nag screen plays into the users' impulse buy mentality. Once users have downloaded and opened up your free app, you can offer that premium content and expect a reasonable conversion rate. Make sure that you don't throw just anything up there. Like any upsell, you do have to be strategic in how and what you promote to your customers. A slick demonstration of value on a nag screen may hook potential buyers, but, if done improperly, it can turn customers away from your app entirely.

Nag screens are usually used to upsell from a free version of an app to its pro version but you can use them to advertise one of your other apps

FIGURE 8.1 Nag screen example.

as well. You can even promote your other free apps to grow your app network. After all, who wouldn't like to get another one of your free apps, especially if they're enjoying the one they have?

Nag screens have two styles. One is the default blue nag screen, which looks like all the other alerts you get on your phone. This version is easy to implement and good for getting started. When you generate more revenue, you can move to a better looking nag screen, one that fills the screen and is graphically more engaging (see Figure 8.2). On average, these advanced nag screens receive about three times more click-throughs than the default ones.

Nag screens have been the most critical advanced marketing strategy for my business. You have to utilize them. You might think, "I don't want to annoy my users with these ads," and that is a valid thought, but think of this as adding value for users. If they have downloaded your

FIGURE 8.2   Advanced nag screen.

free app and are using it, you have users who are interested in your apps and in that type of app. They might want to get the pro version with the additional features. For those who don't, a quick pop-up message is a small price to pay for using your free app.

You have to accept this and not shy away from this type of marketing. If you're still on the fence, consider this: When Apple launched its iBooks app, it used a nag screen within the App Store app. If you had an iPhone at the time, you may remember seeing that pop-up inviting you to download iBooks. Well, you were nagged by the one and only Apple.

With my free Phone Security app, I was getting around 30,000 downloads a day without generating much revenue. To address this, I added a nag screen to get consumers to upgrade to the pro version. This added around $650 a day immediately. I was converting about 3 percent of the daily free traffic into sales of my paid app. This had such a profound effect that my paid ranking moved up the rankings from 280 to 26, which created more visibility and, ultimately, sales. This upward positive spiral was all fueled by the nag screen on my free app. This is the power of the app network.

When adding a nag screen, explain to your developer what you are looking for, and reference specific examples of other apps that have nag screens. Be sure you can change the nag screen without submitting a new update to the app store. To do this, tell the developer you want your nag screen to be dynamic. That way you can change the marketing message and the app you're advertising at any time. This will allow you to redirect your app network traffic within seconds. This is an absolute must. Your nag screens will lose a huge part of their effectiveness if you cannot change them on the fly.

For this to happen, the developer must implement something called a server-client interaction so every time the app launches, it checks in with the server and gets the latest version of the nag screen. You'll be able to edit your nag screen on the server, and your app will show the new version of your nag screen. Your developer should be able to understand this concept and create the dynamic nag screens you're looking for. You also need to be able to turn off your nag screens and turn them back on.

Keep your nag screens simple, short, and benefit-oriented. The amount of space you have is limited. Maximize the impact of your message by focusing on the benefits of the app you're promoting. It's crucial to include a call to action as well as seen in Figure 8.1.

How do you assess the effectiveness of your nag screen? All you have to do is keep track of how many times you show a particular nag screen as opposed to how many of those users click on "yes" to check out the app you're promoting. This is called your click-through rate, and the higher the percentage the better.

Special promotions usually receive higher click-through rates. "Upgrade now before the price goes back up" or "Free only for a few days so get it now" are useful calls to action. You should test and change your nag screen message on a regular basis to see if can get better click-through rates. Track all of this activity with Flurry so you can make informed decisions on what nag screen copy converts the best.

Add nag screens to all of your apps, even the paid ones. You should not turn on the nag screens of your paid apps because that will really annoy your users. But you never know when you might decide to make one of your paid apps free for a certain amount of time. You want to freedom to turn that app's nag screen on and direct its traffic to another app in your app network, especially if it takes off and starts generating lots of traffic. If you don't, you could lose out on a lot of money.

PROMO PAGES

If the nag screen is your most important cross-promotion tool, your promo page will be your second most important (see Figure 8.3). Unlike the nag screen, you can cross-promote more than one app at a time, and that is the power of the promo page. This is essentially a section of your app that lists all of your other apps and the apps of the developers with whom you're cross-promoting.

FIGURE 8.3   Promo page example.

The promo page example shows several apps covering the entire page. Users are able to scroll down to see more listed apps. Keep this page simple like the nag screen. Only include the icon, title, and a short description of the apps that you are promoting. Make sure your short description is enticing, and avoid clutter at all costs. You need to have an arrow at the right side of each app. This shows users they will get more information when they touch the banner, and it's a subtle call to action.

Each one of those banners links to the promoted app. When users touch the banner, they are taken to the App Store to review and download that app. This is a powerful tool to further increase sales. I've tested several color schemes for the promo page and have found that the bright gray and dark gray banner background color scheme of the App Store works best. I recommend you do the same if you want to maximize the click-through rates of your promo pages.

Each one of the banner positions of your promo page will be worth a certain amount of money based on the daily traffic of your app. The higher the banner position, the more money it is worth because it gets more visibility and thus users click on it more often. For example, if one of your apps is getting 10,000 downloads a day, you can assume that a certain number of your users will enter your promo page. Let's say 25 percent of the 10,000, which is 2,500 users. If you can generate sales from only 10 percent of those users who have entered your promo page, you will have another 250 sales, which is about $175. And that's from the promo page of only one of your apps.

You might wonder how to direct people to the promo pages in your apps. Every one of your apps needs to have a button with the word "More" on it prominently displayed in the main page or menu section inside of your app. (See Figures 8.4 and 8.5.) That's all. I've tested many other promo button labels like "More apps," "I," or "+," but "More" had the greatest click-through rates. When users hit the more button, they are taken to my promo page, which has a back button to return them to where they were before.

Your More button must be highly visible. One way to do this is to give it some bright color or a glow effect to draw your users' attention. You might think you don't want to be too aggressive with your advertising, but remember the nag screen discussion above. You have to get some traffic on your promo page so you can show your users all the other cool apps that you or others have created.

FIGURE 8.4   Example of a More button.

Some developers decide to be more subtle and place the promo page button hidden somewhere where users have to move through several pages to see it. Another issue is that the promo page button sometimes blends in too much and doesn't grab the users' attention. If you're going to do that, then you might as well not have a promo page because you will be diminishing its effect. Your users must see it as soon as they open the app.

The reason why it's so important to get a lot of traffic to your promo page is because, along with the nag screen, your promo page is where all your app network magic happens. Each banner that's linking to another one of your apps in your promo page is creating a link between those two apps. The sum of these links will make up your app network. So, link away, my fellow appreneur.

FIGURE 8.5 Another example of a More button.

How do you set up a promo page? The concept is similar to the nag screen. Whoever sets up your nag screen should create your promo pages, so you'll have an integrated system.

Your promo page will be a useful tool to cross-promote with other developers. The reason you want to cross-promote with others is this can increase the number of people who see your apps. Your apps will be visible to your own app network and to the app network of the developers you're cross-promoting with. How do you do it? Throw their apps on your promo pages and ask them to do the same for you. Instant traffic boost.

The concept of cross-promotion is not unique to the app business. In real estate, every agent is taught at the beginning of their career to network with people who provide services for the home buying process. For example, you build relationships with mortgage brokers, and they send you people looking for houses. In return, you send them people looking for loans.

With Alan, I immediately saw how this applied to the app world and decided to cross-promote my apps with him. But I didn't stop there. I got in touch with other entertainment app companies including Lima Sky, the creators of Doodle Jump. It was great timing because they were releasing their new Bubble Wrap app. I was able to get them to cross-promote with me and this increased the amount of traffic to my app network.

If you model this strategy with several developers, instead of one, you have the potential of seeing your traffic skyrocket. Find developers whose apps have similar amounts of traffic and similar demographics to your own and maximize your conversion rate. Utility apps, for example, will not cross-promote as well to games as they do to other utility apps because the demographic differs.

PUSH NOTIFICATIONS

Push notifications are another effective advanced marketing tactic. A push notification sends a message to customers who have your app on their phone. The notification can contain whatever message you want to pass on to the user. It pops up on the screen like a text message, requiring the user to discard the message or to open the app that has sent it. The ingenuity of push notifications is that you're reminding users of your app and giving them the option to open it up with a touch of the screen.

Since these notifications are displayed like text messages, the open rate is close to 100 percent. After all, have you ever not read a text message that popped up on your screen? That's huge for marketing your app and untouched by any other type of advertising in any industry.

Push notifications are a powerful in-your-face way of marketing your app and have to be used tactfully. Don't send push notifications every day because customers will get annoyed and delete your app. It's one thing to show them some advertising when they are actively engaged with one of your apps, but it's different to send them a push notification, interrupting whatever else they may be doing at that time.

This strategy works best after you've built a solid fan base that is excited to use your apps or to see what your next update will be. The company Outfit7, with their hugely successful Talking Tom and other "talking apps," do a great job with this. They rarely send push notifications and when they do it's something fun like "I miss you" or "Come play with me." Sometimes they also advertise a new feature.

Let's consider the financial impact of push notifications. Assume you have an app that has an active user base of 250,000. If you send out a push notification and only 10 percent of your users check it out, you will have infused your app network with an additional 25,000 users for that particular day. That traffic will increase your revenue through additional sales, banner clicks, and affiliate income. It's like printing money with the click of button.

YOUR DEVELOPER NETWORK

A few months after its release, my top app started dropping in the rankings, and I didn't know how to stop it. I asked myself: "What can I do to make this a sustainable business rather than a one-hit wonder?" So, I thought, "Whom do I know in this business who can help me? Who can be a mentor? Who can I model for success?" That was what I had always thought of when I wanted to take things to the next level.

The reality was that I didn't know anybody in the business. The app industry was so new at the time that most developers were concentrated in Silicon Valley, so that's where I decided to go. I landed in San Francisco with everything I owned in two bags. I was dedicated, ready to network and start my life as an appreneur. My cross-country move propelled my business to new heights. The first contact I made was Alan, and from there my developer network took off. I networked with other appreneurs and learned the strategies they were using to monetize their apps. I never would have thought of some of these on my own.

You don't have to uproot your life and move to San Francisco to network since developers are everywhere and you can leverage technology. But your success depends on finding like-minded people to network with. Learning from somebody who's doing well can help you make progress faster than figuring out the ins and outs of the business yourself.

Where can you find them? Use Meetup (appempire.com/meetup) or similar networking sites, industry conferences, developer blogs, and so on. Meetup connects you with people in similar industries or with similar hobbies. At the first iPhone developer meet-up I went to, I met a few great developers, and they introduced me to their developer friends. We created a mastermind group that became pivotal to our success. They taught me their skills, and I was able to show them a few things to help them take their businesses to the next level.

Motivated by the results of the mastermind group, I attended app conferences and grew my developer network. These conferences are a networker's dream, allowing appreneurs to learn new, useful information and meet like-minded people. One time, I went to the BizTech conference, where Internet marketing expert and app developer Joel Comm was speaking. At the end of his speech, I asked Mr. Comm a question and began by introducing myself and plugging my app in front of a large crowd of attendees.

Afterward, several people came over to me and said, "I'm an app developer, too." It was a great way to meet people, but I had to put myself out there first.

The good news is that you don't have to get up and talk in front of a crowd of hundreds to network successfully. When you attend meet-ups and technology conferences, introduce yourself to people one at a time and ask questions to find out more. Ask where they are from, what they do, and so on. Everybody is there to learn and meet others so you don't need to be shy. For every conference you go to, make it your goal to bring one person into your "inner circle." Before you know it, you'll have a dream team appreneur network.

Another good way to connect and learn from other developers is developer blogs. Now that the app industry is growing in leaps and bounds, many developers are creating blogs to talk about their successes. I recommend checking them out and contacting a few. Make comments on their blogs and ask questions. You can contact other people who post comments on their sites to see what they are working on. It's another opportunity to network and share ideas. A single new connection can lead to an influx of revenue for your business and, who knows, a new friendship.

Work on your developer network as much as you're working on your app network.

UPDATES

Guess what. There is no such thing as a finished app. You'll be fixing bugs, adding new features, or responding to competition on a consistent basis. To get the newest version of your app to your users, all you have to do is upload it to Apple for review, much like the first time you publish your app. After Apple's approval, all users who have your app installed on their device will see that an update is available (see Figure 8.6). This seems simple and obvious but updates are a huge marketing opportunity.

FIGURE 8.6   App updates on the App Store app.

When you push out an update, a portion of your users will download this new version of your app. Based on your user base, the number of people downloading your update could surpass your regular daily traffic. I've seen many updates that increased my daily traffic by 5 to 10 times. So, if you have 10,000 downloads per day, your update could add 50,000 to 100,000 additional downloads that day. These will not count for your ranking and not every user opens up your app after an update, but your daily traffic can double even if a small percentage of users decides to check out your update. This will cause a spike in your income and remind the users about your app.

Update frequently for any reason you can think of. Don't wait to for your programmer to add 10 features to submit and update. It's better to submit 10 updates, one for each feature as you build them out. Your users won't mind and will get the impression you are constantly improving your app. I consider updates free advertising because you capture a percentage of the users who download the update to see what features have been added.

So, keep in mind: Updates = Dollars.

PAID TRAFFIC

Another advanced strategy you can use is to pay for traffic to grow your app network quickly. A few companies have specialized in getting massive amounts of traffic for your apps. Some of the big names are FreeAppADay (appempire.com/freeappaday) and TapJoy (appempire .com/tapjoy). FreeAppADay will promote your app to its large user database if you offer your paid app free for a limited time. You pay a fee to the company for the traffic it sends you. I used it to promote my Alarm Security app, which had been ranked number 180 in the utilities category and was getting about 1,000 downloads a day. I spent $2,500 to get the FreeAppADay traffic. The app shot up in the rankings to number 17 overall, increasing the traffic to about 40,000 a day. This helped me to grow my app network and increase my overall income. As the app world grows, look for more and more of these companies to pop up. Only use this strategy if it makes economic sense, but exhaust all of the free tactics first.

Now that you have learned how to build your app network, let's find out how to squeeze the most amount of dollars from it in the next chapter.

What I Learned

1.
2.
3.

Actions to Take

1. Add nag screens to your app.
2. Add more buttons and promo pages to cross-promote your apps.
3. Add push notifications to your apps.
4. Network with other app developers on a regular basis.
5. Update your apps on a regular basis.
6. Consider paid options to grow your app network.

9

Show Me the Money!

Monetizing Your Apps

Money can't buy happiness but neither can poverty.

—Leo Rosten

When I was a kid, I realized pretty quickly that I needed more money than the small allowance I was getting every week for making my bed. Like most 10-year-olds, I wanted to buy things like baseball cards and an awesome shiny red bike I had seen in a magazine.

School was out for the summer and since my cousin had similar aspirations as me, we decided to sell lemonade from a stand on the sidewalk with hopes of making some money. We were two cute little kids selling lemonade for a dollar a cup and we thought that we were going to be an instant hit.

To our surprise, we didn't make that much money. Setting up the stand and making all those drinks ended up being a lot of work. We were determined and we kept at it for a few weeks before we realized there had to be a better way. If we were ever going to get those amazing bikes, we needed to make some changes, and make them quickly.

First, we tried charging two dollars per cup thinking that would make us more money; that actually made us less money because fewer people were buying. Next, we changed the time of day when we were selling the lemonade, figuring that we'd get the most amount of buyers around five o'clock when people were getting off work. This move did increase the number of people stopping by, and we started to sell more lemonade. Unfortunately, we still had the same problem. Selling cups of lemonade was not making us nearly as much money as we had anticipated because people were spending $1 and leaving. Things were moving too slowly, and we felt deflated and completely frustrated. What were we doing wrong? Were we not that cute after all?

On the day our short-lived careers as lemonade entrepreneurs were about to end, we had an aha moment. We realized that most of our customers were stopping by before they headed to the grocery store to pick up food for dinner.

This gave us an idea. We were doing well drawing people in but it seemed that we were not able to get the people who were stopping by to spend much money. Selling lemonade alone wasn't going to make us enough money to buy those bikes. If we could sell them some of the food they were going to buy at the grocery store, we could make money faster.

Luckily, my family had a big garden with more veggies than we could eat. All we needed to do was to pick them. Bingo. We immediately changed our game plan and offered free lemonade to attract more customers so we could sell them the produce from our garden. It worked perfectly. People stopped by, grabbed some free lemonade, and bought veggies. It was great, everyone was happy, and let me tell you, I had a blast riding that bike all summer long.

Looking back at those early days, I realize that after some trial and error, my cousin and I had discovered how to optimize and fully monetize our traffic, a skill that is essential in business. Whether you are working a lemonade stand or running a big company, you need to be flexible and constantly look for new ways to monetize your business. Here is the crucial question you should be asking yourself every day: "How else can I further monetize my traffic?"

Nine months after launching my app business, I was getting around 30,000 downloads a day with my free and paid apps. That brought roughly $650 a day in revenue. After learning about and deciding to try several new monetization tactics, I took that same 30,000 downloads and turned it into about $2,200 a day in revenue. That's a 238 percent increase.

Utilizing the same traffic I had before, I was able to bring in more money because I understood how to monetize my apps in multiple ways. Some of the main monetization techniques I use are regular paid app sales, banner advertising, affiliate marketing, in-app purchases, and translations (all discussed later in this chapter). All of these techniques, once implemented, will increase your revenue without any additional work. This is money sitting on the table and all you have to do is reach out and grab it.

THE THREE REVENUE MODELS

The App Store has three major revenue models. They include the free model, the premium model, and the freemium model. A common misconception among developers is that you can only make money with paid apps. You have plenty of ways to generate revenue from free and freemium apps as well, and oftentimes these last two models are easier to monetize.

When I first got into the business, I didn't know that multiple ways to make money existed. I used the paid model, pricing my apps at 99 cents.

As the monetization models evolved, I had to adapt. I created many free apps and some freemium apps. This is what you should do as well. Don't focus on generating revenue from one model but maximize your gains from each one of them. Let's take a closer look at the three revenue models.

Free Model. When the App Store opened, most of the available apps were paid, so when I jumped in, I thought it would be crazy to give apps away for free. Now, developers have to provide free apps to keep up with the competition.

Free apps can be fully functional, but they often are lite versions of their full-featured counterparts. The "try it before you buy it" strategy is an old business concept, and most developers offer free, versions of their apps that have fewer features to upsell to their pro versions.

We've discussed the importance of free apps previously but we need to mention them again because they will be the bread and butter of your monetization strategy. Free apps serve many purposes. They are the main source of traffic for your app network, they are your main cross-promotion tool (using nag screens and promo pages), and they can be easily and lucratively monetized using banner advertising, affiliate marking, and translations.

Premium Model. The premium model includes all paid apps on the App Store and you make money when a user purchases your app. In contrast to free apps, consumers must buy before they try. This can be a deterrent, which is why it is a good idea to simultaneously offer ad-supported lite versions of your paid app. The initial sale is not the only way to monetize premium apps. You can monetize them more with affiliate marketing, in-app purchases, and translations. You have to have paid apps because you're going to want to direct a lot of your app network traffic toward them.

Freemium Model. The freemium model is a hybrid of the free and premium model. These free apps have optional paid content (in-app purchases). The idea is, like with free apps, the users can try before they buy. But unlike free apps, instead of sending the user back to the app store to review and buy a paid app, freemium apps have the premium content included in the app, which can be unlocked and used with an in-app purchase. This is powerful because a freemium app provides the traffic-generation power of free apps with the sales benefit of premium apps. Essentially, they allow you to have your cake and eat it, too.

BANNER ADVERTISING

As the number of customers with smart phones increases, more advertisers are switching to mobile advertising to reach their target audiences (Figure 9.1). As intermediaries, mobile ad networks handle the sales and placement of mobile ads. Advertisers can buy ad space from the ad networks and developers can use their apps to display the ads. The advertisers benefit from the sales that result from their ads, and you, the developer, earn revenue from the ads. The ad networks keep 40 percent, and the developers receive 60 percent of the proceeds from advertising revenue generated from this process.

If you have a smartphone, you probably have seen ads on the top or bottom of your screen inside of an app before. The developers of

FIGURE 9.1   Example of banner advertising.

those apps are making money every time one of those ads is displayed or clicked on. You should take banner ads seriously as they can be a major income source.

For example, a top-10 free app can make at least $500 a day from displaying banner ads alone. Granted, not all of your apps will be in the top ten, but even if you're generating $50 a day per app with only three apps, you'll be making some serious cash with ads. That's around $150 a day or $4,500 a month or $54,000 a year. It's a good deal for only having to dedicate a small space in your app for ads and not having to do any more work.

The terms used in banner advertising can seem like a big bowl of alphabet soup at first. Let's take a look at some of the most common ones. You don't have to know these to make money with ads but they can help later when you're maximizing your banner ad gains.

- *Impressions:* Whenever one of your apps displays an ad to users, you have "served" one ad impression. Impressions are usually low revenue generators because it's unclear if the users saw the ad or paid attention to it. This is more of a shotgun approach where advertisers pay for lots of impressions and hope the ads will catch some of the users' attention.
- *Clicks:* A click occurs every time users click (or touch) an ad. Advertisers are willing to pay a premium for receiving clicks since that means consumers are showing genuine interest in the ad.
- *Fill Rate:* Advertising networks are not always able to supply developers with ads. Your fill rate is essentially the percentage of times your app received an ad when it made a request to the ad network server. The optimal fill rate is 100 percent.
- *CPM or cost-per-mille (thousand):* The price that advertisers pay ad networks in exchange for 1,000 ad impressions.
- *CPC or cost-per-click:* The price that advertisers pay ad networks in exchange for consumers clicking their ad.
- *CTR or click-through-rate:* The number of times consumers click ads relative to the number of times they see it (impressions).
- *eCPM or effective cost-per-mille:* The revenue your application generates per 1,000 ad impressions, calculated by the following formula: [total earnings / impressions] ×1000.
- *eCPC or effective cost-per-click:* The same as eCPM. Instead of impressions, this measures clicks. Given that clicks generate more revenue than impressions, eCPC will be higher than eCPM.

Some of the top advertising networks that allow you to place ads in your apps are Apple's iAd, Google's AdMob, and Millennial Media. Many others exist, but these three are good ones to start with.

So, which one should you use? Use all of them because that will allow you to maximize your fill rate. As mentioned above, ad networks don't always serve an ad when your app requests one. This means you're missing out on income each time your app tries to show an ad but cannot. When not all of your ad requests are being filled, your fill rate is less than 100 percent. You cannot do much about this when you're working only with one ad network. Each network will serve whatever ads it has available and that's it. But what if you could request ads from multiple networks, switching from one to the other anytime your request does not result in an ad? That could guarantee a 100 percent fill rate and, therefore, maximize your banner ad income.

Each of these platforms is designed to be used separately. If you wanted to use them all, your programmer would have to interface with each one of them and create the logic that would alternate between. You could do this, but that's extra programming.

So, how do you request ads from multiple ad networks? Use AdWhirl.

AdWhirl (appempire.com/adwhirl) is a service (owned by Google) that allows you to integrate more than one ad network into your apps and seamlessly handles the distribution of your ad requests. Whenever one of your apps does not get an ad when it asks for it, AdWhirl redirects that request to another ad network based on your preferences. Once you link three or four ad networks to your AdWhirl account, you will have 100 percent fill rates consistently without doing any additional work.

I was initially only using iAds, but my apps were getting 10–50 percent fill rates. After I found out about AdWhirl and had it implemented in all my apps, my ad network revenue tripled. I could have done this sooner, but I didn't know about it. That's where your developer networks and masterminds will come in handy. They will help you discover techniques like these much faster.

AdWhirl is useful because you have full control over everything. You can assign ad request percentages to the ad networks. (See Figure 9.2.) You might want 50 percent of your request to go to iAd, 25 percent to AdMob, and the remaining 25 percent to Millennial Media. Or you can evenly distribute your requests among all of them. You choose.

This is great because you can send more ad requests to the networks that make you the most money. You can turn off certain networks if you

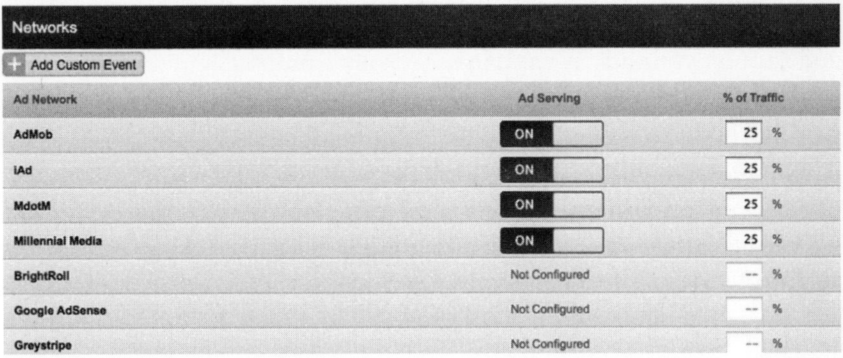

FIGURE 9.2   Distributing ad traffic on AdWhirl.

FIGURE 9.3   Selecting backfill priority on AdWhirl.

don't want any ad requests to be sent to them. You'll always have the option to turn them back on.

You can also select the backfill priority of your ad request. (See Figure 9.3.) That means you decide the order in which AdWhirl should request ads from other ad networks if the current network did not return an ad. This level of control will allow you to extract the most amount of money from your banner advertising.

Another cool feature of AdWhirl is you can have in-house ads. That means, you can advertise your own apps within your own banner ads. All you have to do is upload a nice-looking banner of your app and the link for it. Then you decide what percent of the time you want your own ad to be displayed and there you go. Your ad will appear with ads of the other ad networks and your users won't be able to tell the difference.

One thing I like doing is adding AdWhirl to my paid apps as well. Like with your nag screen, you'll want to turn off banner ads in a paid app.

But if you ever decided to do a FreeAppADay promotion and make your paid app free for a limited amount of time, you can jump on AdWhirl and turn on your ads to capitalize on your temporarily free traffic. This could make you thousands of extra dollars. You have to give yourself that flexibility to monetize all your apps at all times.

As for how to integrate AdWhirl, like with your nag screen and promo pages, your programmers need to be experienced with this. Let them handle all the details and check that everything is working before you submit the app.

AFFILIATE MARKETING

Affiliate marketing is relatively widespread on the Internet and many people are still making lots of money with it. The basic concept is that if people have something to sell online, they give you a certain percentage of any sale generated by customers you brought to their website. You (the affiliate) are getting a commission from sellers for connecting them with buyers.

If I were selling a $100 audio course on how to make iPhone apps, I could decide that I want to give 50 percent of the sales to my affiliates. You might be a developer who has a blog on how to make iPhone apps and you might like my product. You decide to put an ad on your blog that promotes my product. Lots of people visit your site daily, and some of them will see your ad, click on it, and be directed to my site. Some of those people who clicked on your ad will buy my product. For every person that comes from your site and buys my product, you would be entitled to 50 percent or $50 dollars.

That's cool because you would be making money from a product that you didn't create. Furthermore, you have users (traffic) on your website so why not show them something that might interest them and make some money at the same time? The seller knows the traffic came from you because each affiliate gets a unique identifying link, called the affiliate link. That way no confusion occurs about where users came from and all affiliates get what they are entitled to.

Affiliate marketing has been around since the beginning of the Internet. Thousands of products on the Internet are being promoted by affiliates. As a result, there are websites that serve as intermediaries between the sellers and the affiliates. The sellers posts their products and the commission amount, and affiliates can browse through these offers and pick the ones they find most lucrative or relevant to their traffic. One such website is LinkShare (appempire.com/linkshare).

LinkShare connects sellers with affiliates. It also serves as an affiliate sales tracking service. Once you sign up as an affiliate with LinkShare, you can find the links you need to use to promote certain products. After you start promoting those products, you can log into LinkShare any time and see detailed statistics on how much revenue your traffic is generating for the seller. (See Figure 9.4.) You can see how much money you have made from those sales. LinkShare collects your earnings from the seller and sends them to you on a regular basis, which is simple and effective.

So, why are we talking about all this affiliate mumbo jumbo if all of this action is happening on the Internet? We are because affiliate marketing also exists on smartphones. Apple is one of the biggest sellers of digital content on the Internet and as such it has partnered with LinkShare to offer a commission to any affiliate that sends it customers who purchase their movies, songs, digital books, and apps. What does that mean in practical terms? Any affiliate that directs traffic to Apple's iTunes store is entitled to 5 percent of any purchase the users make for the next 72-hour period.

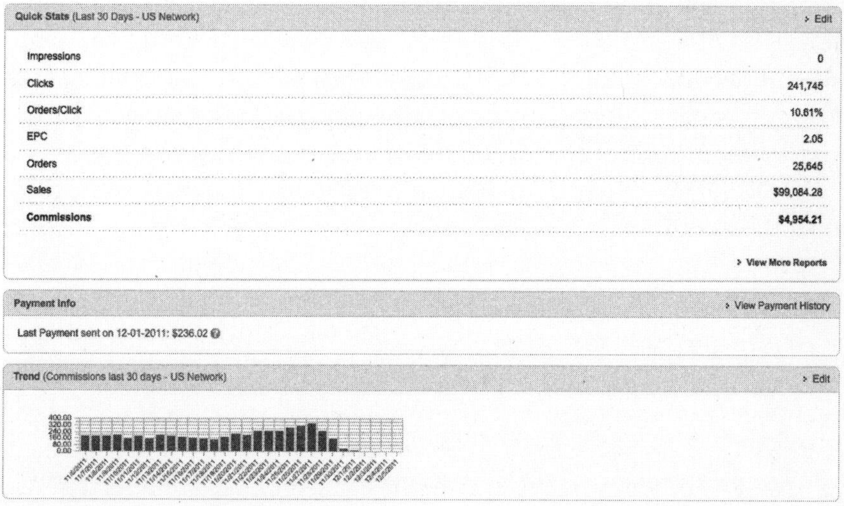

FIGURE 9.4   LinkShare reporting.

You should care because you are in the business of building apps and directing traffic using your app network. Anytime one of your users clicks on your nag screens or promo page banners, you are sending them to the App Store. The stronger your app network becomes, the more traffic you will be sending on a daily basis to Apple and the more affiliate revenue you will be generating.

All you have to do is sign up with LinkShare and use the correct affiliate link that will attribute to you the traffic you send to Apple. You're linking people to your apps anyway, so use a LinkShare affiliate link and start collecting that affiliate commission that you deserve. (See Figure 9.5.)

Here is an example of a regular iTunes link:

http://itunes.apple.com/us/app/fingerprint-security-pro/id312912865
    ?mt=8

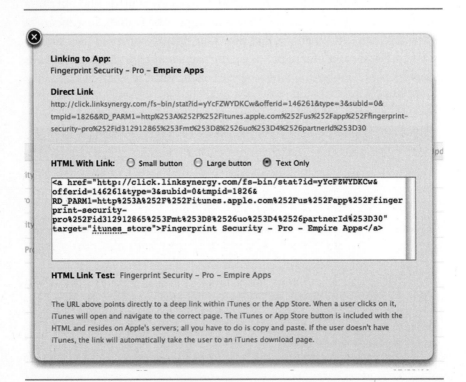

FIGURE 9.5   Creating affiliate links.

Here is an example of a LinkShare affiliate link:

http://click.linksynergy.com/fs-bin/click?id=LjQr0YBXPSs&subid=&
offerid=146261.1&type=10&tmpid=3909&RD_PARM1=http%
3A%2F%2Fitunes.apple.com%2Fus%2Fapp%2Ffingerprint-security
-pro%2Fid312912865% 3Fmt%3D8

Don't be intimidated by the size of the affiliate link. Remember that
LinkShare will create it for you, and all you have to do is copy and paste
that particular link instead of the first one. Your programmer is the one who
is going to handle all of this anyway. Both links will direct you to the same
app, but one gets you paid, and the other does not. Even if users you direct
to iTunes don't buy any of your apps, you will still make money from any
other apps or digital content they buy over the next 72 hours. That's a
great return for such a small additional time investment.

Unfortunately most developers don't know about affiliate marketing
or choose to ignore it. Affiliate marketing is huge. How huge, you ask?
For the three companies I owned, affiliate marketing made up 15 percent
of overall revenue. One month, it was as high as $110,000. Just for using
affiliate links rather than regular links. I'm still blown away by that.

One thing to keep in mind with affiliate marketing is that the links
you create are country specific. Apple has decided to use LinkShare for
the United States and Canada. You have to use a different link for each
one of these countries. For Europe, Apple has chosen to partner with
LinkShare's European counterpart, which is TradeDoubler (appempire
.com/tradedoubler). For Australia and New Zealand, Apple has partnered
with DGM (appempire.com/dgmpro). Initially, you can stick to using
U.S. LinkShare links because the United States has the largest app market. Once you gain some traction with your apps, you'll want your
apps to be aware of the country they are being used in. That way you
can use the correct affiliate link for each country and collect the affiliate
commission you otherwise would not.

Set up international affiliate marketing links because your international
traffic could be half of your app network traffic. That was the case for
me. It took me some time to set the international affiliate links, and during that time, I was leaving money on the table, similar to not getting 100
percent fill rates with my banner ads. Your programmer will know how
to handle this and again it might be best to make this part of your server
backend and have an integrated system.

IN-APP PURCHASES

When the App Store first opened, you couldn't sell content to the user from within the apps. You could only pay for an app when you purchased it or could download the app free. At some point, Apple saw the need for a system that would allow developers to sell content within their apps, and it created in-app purchases FYI: look out for any changes like this because they mean $$.

The concept is as simple as the name implies. Developers can sell various items inside of their apps. Users select the item and get a prompt that reads something like "Do you want to purchase this xyz feature for 99 cents?" If users agree, they have to enter their iTunes account password, as when purchasing apps on the App Store. Whatever content users have purchased unlocks or becomes available in the app (Figure 9.6).

FIGURE 9.6 Example of an in-app purchase notification.

The beauty of the in-app purchases is that they are seamless. Apple still handles the financial transaction as with regular app sales and users never have to leave the app. This is great for the users because they can get additional functionality after they ensure they like the app. It's great for developers because they can make lots of extra cash while keeping users engaged, and it's great for Apple because it still gets 30 percent of each transaction. It's a win-win-win.

Consequently, in-app purchases have changed the landscape of app monetization. While most developers were focusing on making money with paid apps, they began to offer more free apps with paid content in them. In-app purchases created the freemium model, which is the primary revenue model many developers utilize. If you look at the top 25 overall grossing apps on the App Store, you will see that at least half of them are

FIGURE 9.7   Example of several in-app purchases in one app.

free. That means the 12–15 apps that are making the most money in the App Store are generating their revenue solely with in-app purchases.

In-app purchases are particularly popular in games. Usually, users can play the game without any restrictions, but if they want to progress faster or use fun add ons, they can get them with in-app purchases. It seems unlikely but many people pay for virtual items. Some utility apps offer additional content or functionality with in-app purchases as well. When I released my Emoji app, I decided to make it a freemium app and give users the option to purchase additional emojis with an in-app purchase. That strategy paid off handsomely. (See Figure 9.7.)

When it comes to in-app purchases, it's up to your imagination what you might offer. Anything you can think of that your users might want and would pay for can be in your app as an in-app purchase.

	..ıl.. AT&T 3G	11:10 PM	86%
	Info	Top In-App Purchases	
3	Bag of Gems		$9.99
4	Pile of Cash		$0.99
5	Pile of Food		$0.99
6	Sack of Food		$1.99
7	Sack of Cash		$1.99
8	Bag of Food		$4.99
9	Bag of Cash		$4.99
10	Box of Gems		$24.99

Featured   Categories   Top 25   Search   Updates (58)

FIGURE 9.8   Top in-app purchases.

The other cool thing is that you can offer as many in app purchases as you like, and depending on the value of the item, the in-app purchase can have a high price. Users that would have never paid $15 to purchase an app have no problem paying that amount inside an app they like, especially if they want that additional item, feature, or content. (See Figure 9.8.)

When it comes to app monetization, you must use in-app purchases whenever you can. Always figure out what content and feature you could turn into an in-app purchase to create more user value. If you have an app generating a lot of traffic, some of those users will want more from your app. It makes sense to utilize the traffic you have to make more money. Let's consider some numbers. Assume you have an app with 10,000 downloads per day. If only 2 percent of your users decided to get your in-app purchase, you would have 200 extra sales and make another $140 per day.

The nice thing is that you can do this without having any negative impact on your app. Users who don't want the additional content will continue using your app the way they did, and users who want more content will be happy they can get it. It doesn't get better than this. By the way, your app doesn't have to be free for you to offer in-app purchases. You could have your paid apps offering in-app purchases. Many games do this as well.

Integrating in-app purchases will increase your development cost a little. The return on investment is usually really good. Plan it before development like the rest of your apps and let your programmers know about it. They'll handle the rest.

TRANSLATING YOUR APPS

One of the best ways to monetize your apps more is to increase their global visibility. This requires translating your marketing components (title, description, keywords, screenshots) into different languages, which is also called localization. This allows people in other countries to find your apps using their language. This also allows them to understand all of your marketing components, which increases your international traffic and revenue.

The great thing about this is that you don't have to localize for specific countries. You only have to localize for languages because when you add a certain language, such as Spanish, your app will show up in Spanish for all of the Spanish-speaking countries. That's powerful. (See Figures 9.9 and 9.10.)

App Store > Utilities > Empire Apps

Alarm Security - Pro

Description

++++++++++
VERIZON LAUNCH SPECIAL: 99 CENTS!!
GET IT NOW BEFORE THE PRICE GOES BACK UP!!
++++++++++

****
THE MOST AMAZING ALARM SYSTEM FOR YOUR IPHONE/IPOD
****

Stop any thief, friend, or parent in their tracks !!

Alarms Security will sound one of the over 20 alarms provided by the app if anybody moves your iPhone or iPod Touch.

You can also record your own alarms sounds. Some of sounds included are:

Self destruct initiated, police sirens, fire truck sirens, intruder alert, battle stations, chimpanzee, elephant, dog, fireworks, crying baby and many more!!

Stop a thief or just prank your friends.

You will not be let down !!Get Alarm Security and see for yourself !!

Empire Apps Web Site >   Alarm Security - Pro Support >

Downloaded ▾

Category: Utilities
Updated: Oct 21, 2011
Version: 3.8
Size: 7.1 MB
Language: English
Seller: The Empire Group LLC
© 2010 Empire Apps

Rated 9+ for the following:
· Infrequent/Mild Horror/Fear Themes
· Infrequent/Mild Cartoon or Fantasy
  Violence

FIGURE 9.9   Alarm Security description in English.

App Store > Dienstprogramme > Empire Apps

Sicherheitsalarm Handy Schutz und Bildschirm Sperre (Alarm Security Phone Protection and Screen Lock)

Beschreibung

****
DIE AUSSERGEWÖHNLICHSTE ALARMANLAGE FÜR DEIN IPHONE/IPOD
****

Stoppt jeden Dieb, Freund oder deine Eltern !!

Der Sicherheitsalarm ertönt sobald jemand dein iPhone oder iPod Touch auch nur berührt. Dabei greift die App auf mehr als 20 unterschiedliche Alarmgeräusche zurück. Außerdem kannst du deine eigenen Alarmgeräusche aufnehmen und zum Einsatz bringen. Einige der mitgelieferten Geräusche sind:

Selbstzerstörungssequenz, Polizeisirene, Feuerwehrsirene, Alarmanlage, Gefechtsstationen, Schimpanse, Elefant, Hund, Feuerwerk, schreiendes Baby und viele mehr!!

Stoppe jeden Dieb oder lege deine Freunde herein. Hol dir die Sicherheitsalarm App und überzeug dich selbst!!

Website von Empire Apps >
Sicherheitsalarm Handy Schutz und Bildschirm Sperre (Alarm Security Phone Protection and Screen Lock) Support >

0,79 € App kaufen ▾

Kategorie: Dienstprogramme
Aktualisiert: 21.10.2011
Version: 3.8
Größe: 7.1 MB
Sprache: Englisch
Entwickler: The Empire Group LLC
© 2010 Empire Apps

Freigabe 9+ für Folgendes:
· Selten/schwach ausgeprägt: Horror-
  /Gruselszenen

FIGURE 9.10   Alarm Security description translated into German.

When I was searching for ways to grow my app business, I asked my developers and masterminds what they were doing to take their businesses to the next level. Localization turned out to be a major way to grow traffic and increase revenue with existing apps.

Prior to localizing my apps, most of my time and effort had been spent on the English-speaking markets. Because of that, 80 percent of my revenue came from English-speaking countries, and 20 percent came from the others. I wasn't getting more international traffic because most non-English speakers were not finding my apps and could not understand my marketing because of the language barrier.

After I got the localization tip, I found people in other countries to translate my apps into their languages and updated my apps to get the translations released in the App Store. The first week after my apps were available in other languages, my revenue split went from 80/20 to 60/40. It wasn't because my revenue from English-speaking countries had declined but because my international revenue had increased.

I needed a couple of weeks to implement translations, but I immediately saw the difference the new languages made. Once I added Russian, Spanish, French, German, and Portuguese, to name a few, I saw my income almost double.

One thing to remember is that your app must be successful in the major English-speaking markets (United States, United Kingdom, Canada, and Australia) first before it makes sense to localize it to others. Get it working with your marketing basics first so you have consistent downloads. If it isn't successful in one of these major markets, chances are it's not going to be successful in the rest of the world.

For localization to work, you must make your app easy to find and use for people in other countries. More than that, the translation needs to be appropriate to the culture. People in other countries speak different languages and use words differently. Beyond accurately translating the words to other languages, nuances and colloquialisms will make sense in some languages but not in others. Don't translate on the cheap unless you want to waste time, money, and give yourself a headache. Yes, I speak from experience.

Here are three recommendations for localizing your apps:

1. Find a native of your target language. Use somebody who is a native speaker and not somebody who will run the words through an online translator. I paid a company 400 dollars to translate an app into six languages, one of which was German. After having a German-speaking friend take a look, I discovered the translations were bad. Lots of online services for translations exist. You can find translators by checking out international meet-up groups, foreign language schools, or labs at universities. You can also place an ad on Elance or oDesk.

   For example, I was translating one of our apps that have the word "phone" in it. Apparently, the translation of "cell phone" in German is "Mobiletelefon" or "Funktelefon." These would be proper translations Germans would understand, but nobody uses them. The common term in German is "Handy." If you use a nonnative speaker, you may miss these distinctions, which could mean the difference between having a hit app in that market or not.

2. Determine what works in your target country. Once you have found native speakers, explain a bit about the marketing aspects of the app business. They must understand they are translating marketing copy that needs to be as effective in their language as it is in English. This means their English has to be as good as their native language. Ask them to use terms and phrases common in their language.

   They also need to do a great job when it comes to translating the keywords. People will use these terms to search your apps. A keyword popular in English may not be useful in German and vice versa. The translators must know this and must use keywords best for their language. One good way to get them to understand better is to have them check out the App Store in their native language. They can look at competing apps that have been translated and get a feel for how their translations will be used. They can do keyword research to assist in selecting the right keywords for their language.

3. Translate for the major markets. The App Store is available in over 120 countries. Not all of these countries generate as much revenue as the major ones. Therefore, it wouldn't make sense to translate your apps into every possible language. The idea is to focus on the big dogs first and continue with translations in smaller markets if it makes sense. Currently, the top markets are the United States, China, United Kingdom, Canada, Germany, France, and the Spanish-speaking markets. Always keep an eye on the big markets as well as the emerging ones. Some others will join the ranks of the major ones.

   Translations will put your international app network on hyper speed. Implement them as soon as your apps begin to gain traction.

REINVESTING IN YOUR BUSINESS

As you scale your business and are making money, you must reinvest in your business. You do this by reinvesting in your existing apps and investing in new apps. Spending money to upgrade your apps, offering professional versions, or refreshing their look will increase traffic or keep your existing customers coming back. Many developers miss this step, and therefore, their business hits a plateau.

Investing in new apps will replenish and grow your app network. Remember when I mentioned building a long-term business, a gold mine, rather than creating a one-hit wonder? If you ride your one or two apps, your business will run its course. To create a sustainable app company that makes a lot of money and supports your new lifestyle, you have to keep creating new apps.

One of my developer friends has a rule that his company needs to come up with two new apps every month. Whether he's working or hiking through the mountains of New Zealand, his team is aware of this goal, and it always meets it. Set your own goals for growth and pursue them.

YOUR BACKEND

When I started out, I had only a few apps so it was easy to manage various aspects of my marketing. I changed my nag screens and promo pages manually. I would log on to LinkShare, and grab the affiliate links and so on. This worked well at the beginning, but as I created more apps, manually managing everything consumed more time. Money was coming in, but my head was spinning. I knew a better way existed, so I had a talk with my business partner, and we decided to build software to automate and optimize the entire process.

We needed something that would simplify the management of all of our nag screens and promo pages. We wanted them translated so we could monetize our international traffic more effectively. Ensuring we were getting all of the international affiliate commissions was a high priority. To streamline the entire process, we created a simple database. This database contained all of our nag screens, promo pages with their translations, and all of the correct international affiliate links.

Then we added code to our apps that made them region and language aware. Every time any of our apps is opened, it checks the users' region (country) and language. This information is available in the users' device settings. The app communicates with our backend database and is supplied with the information it needs. If users who have set their region to Germany and their language to French open Fingerprint Security, the app communicates with our server and shows users a French nag screen and French promo pages, but the international affiliate link will be the one for Germany. This process is cool and efficient.

The result of our efforts is what we call the App Empire Network. It adds additional income and I can manage all crucial aspects of my app empire. The reason I mention this is because you'll want to create a back-end system like this eventually, to save time and to improve your bottom line. Check our screenshots on how we set things up at appempire.com/software.

You don't need a setup like this to succeed, especially in the beginning, but a fully integrated backend system can take your business to the next level once you start growing and need to manage lots of apps.

SELLING YOUR APP BUSINESS

One of the biggest, most over-looked ways to cash in on the app gold rush has nothing to do with selling your apps on the App Store. It has to do with selling your turn key app business. Due to the mobile app boom and the potential for strong cash flow with little overhead, many companies all over the world want to acquire app businesses.

They have four reasons for this:

1. It's the hottest industry around.
2. It's more turnkey than most businesses.
3. It's easily scalable, with low overhead.
4. The profit margin of a successful app company is hard to match.

My companies had over 35 million downloads, up to six figures a month of income with an 80 percent profit margin, required me to work only 10 hours a week, and had almost no customer support requests. It is a dream business/life, and everyone wants a piece of it.

So, what can you do to set things up to be attractive to a buyer? Start your business with the goal of selling it in mind. That means keeping good records and automating as much as possible. Set it up to be a turnkey business for potential buyers.

When it's time to sell, use business brokers. They will get a 10 percent commission on the sale, but they will find and screen buyers for you while you are running and growing your business. Before you know it, serious buyers will be lining up at your door. I recommend using AppsRevolution (appempire.com/apprevolution); they are the leading experts at buying and selling app businesses. I used them when I sold Empire Apps and my two other app companies. They handled everything from start to finish without any hiccups.

The amount of money you'll get for your business is going to depend on many factors including your revenue. Some business go for as much as five times their annual revenue, but this will depend on your personal situation. Ask for a good portion of the cash upfront, and maybe even get the rest over time. Doing this will show the buyers you're vested in their success and you won't disappear after training them. This may seem a bit far out for you at the moment, but remember how fast the app business moves. Two of the companies I sold had been in operation for only eight months!

Now that you are a lean, mean monetization machine, you don't want to become a slave to your business as your operations grow. So, let's look at outsourcing and what to monitor next.

What I Learned

1.
2.
3.

Actions to Take

1. Create free, premium, and freemium apps.
2. Create free apps that push traffic to your paid apps.
3. Sign up with AdWhirl, iAd, AdMob, and Millennial Media. Implement AdWhirl in all of your apps to ensure you're getting 100 percent fill rates.
4. Sign up with LinkShare, TradeDoubler, and DGM. Use affiliate marketing links in all of your apps.
5. Add as many in-app purchases into your apps as you can.
6. Translate your marketing material into other languages.
7. Reinvest a certain portion of your revenue in new and existing apps.
8. Once you have many apps, start thinking about an integrated backend.
9. Once your app empire is up and running, consider selling your business.

10

Cruise Control

How to Automate and Monitor Your Business

The price of anything is the amount of life you exchange for it.

—Henry David Thoreau

Bang! Crack! Boom!

The sounds echoed off the lake like cannons shooting from old pirate ships.

"Light it!"

"Run!"

I heard the laughter through the volley of shots piercing the night sky. Sprinting off the dock like a mad man, I made it to where everyone was standing, and dropped down to catch my breath.

I looked up to take in the moment. The professional fireworks I had lined up looked exactly like the ones you usually see in major cities on special occasions. Every extravagant burst sporadically illuminated my 80-year-old grandparents who were watching in awe. Turning right, I saw Matty J., my old high school buddy, and the rest of my family members, smiling from ear to ear, eyes glued to the sky.

Every year since I was 18, I would imagine renting a lakefront camp during the summer and inviting all my friends and family. Year after year, my dream was put on hold because of a lack of funds and time and because of my own doubts. I would get lost in a pile of papers and mindless work thinking no other way existed. Typically, my Fourth of July and holidays were spent working and missing out on the excitement around me that I pretended not to notice.

This year was different. While coming down the mountain from heli-skiing in Whistler, Canada, I remembered that Fourth of July was around the corner. I immediately called my assistant, Super Kate, to find the perfect lakefront camp, and set everything up for my friends and family.

Being able to spend time with my family and friends without distractions from work was priceless. I understood, after all these years, what life was all about. I will never forget the happiness I felt that week.

Even after I had my app business figured out and was making good money, it took me about a year to put a system in place that allowed me to run my business on cruise control while enjoying the lifestyle I had been craving.

Later on that evening, for a second, my thoughts drifted to my app business. I realized I needed to text my programmer to redirect some of our nag screens to our new app, which Apple had approved. He was in Germany at the time, and he made the changes. I completely forgot about it again and continued to enjoy the evening.

The next morning, while lying in bed and going through my numbers on my iPhone, I saw that sales had jumped the previous day by 40 percent to roughly $2,500! It was all from that one move that took two minutes. I was blown away.

Having a reliable and dependable team is liberating. I don't have to be at my business from nine to five because my team members get work done and support me. I can think of ideas spontaneously throughout the day and make them happen even while shooting off fireworks in a random lake half a world away from a team member.

Before setting up my system, I had trouble delegating and outsourcing, and I didn't have an effective way to monitor my business. Once I figured out how to outsource and monitor pivotal areas of my business, everything changed. I was able to track my business, checking stats and managing my team on my iPhone every morning, even when I was on vacation.

In this chapter, I show you ways to do the same thing and put your business on cruise control so you will have time to do what you love in life. That's why we got into this business, remember?

BE DISPENSABLE

By now, you have researched many app ideas, launched a few apps, marketed them, and started making money. The goal is to grow your business without adding more work for yourself. You do this by hiring a team. Your trusted team will help you leverage your time, while you are taking a zip line in Costa Rica, taking your spouse on vacation to Paris, or checking something off your bucket list.

The peace that comes from knowing you can count on others to work on your business when you're away is priceless. Your efforts become more calculated. You spend your time optimizing the areas of your business needing your attention, while maximizing your free time. This efficiency puts you in a more relaxed and positive frame of mind, and work doesn't feel like work anymore. Once you reach this level, you might even have a skip in your step. I know I do.

What I am suggesting is a huge U-turn for many people who feel married to their business or job. Traditional entrepreneurs and businessowners are led to believe this is how it is supposed to be. I fell into this trap myself but to benefit from the app business, you need to relinquish control and divorce yourself from many aspects of your business.

We like to think we're indispensable, but that is true for only certain aspects of your business. The trick is identifying those and allowing yourself to let go and delegate everything else.

When should you start growing your team? At first, like any startup, you'll have to put in some sweat equity and grow as necessary. You will most likely only be working with the programmers you hired to create and manage your first apps. At some point, when your income and workload increase, you will want to scale your business. Saying when that will be is difficult, but I've found that many people wait far too long. They think they should add team members when they have made a lot of money or are making a specific amount of money per month.

I recommend you scale as soon as you can even if this takes away from your bottom line because you can use the additional free time you'll get to double or triple your business income. Another way to decide if you should start hiring is by asking yourself these questions:

- Am I the bottleneck of my business and will hiring someone allow my business to grow faster?
- Am I spending most of my time on little tasks that someone else can do, as opposed to focusing on key aspects?

If the answer to these questions is yes and you've got the funds, it's time scale up so you can spend your time on tasks that will bring in the most amount of money.

SETTING UP YOUR TEAM

The ultimate goal is to hire qualified people you can trust. Do your due diligence and follow the strategies outlined in Chapter 5 for hiring programmers. A lot of them apply to other hires as well. I often start people off part-time. I always give them a one- to three-month test period and let them know this is what I'm doing. If I'm excited about their performance during the test period, I will make them permanent team members. If not, I let them know it is not the right fit and move on.

Your team members' visions must align with yours. If not, those people can sabotage the company, and their discord can spread like a virus. You might have potential hires take a personality test like the Myers-Briggs Type Indicator (MBTI), so you know if the candidate's personality type is compatible with your team. Do not cut corners when hiring people. You can find cheap labor, but that can result in poor quality work or drama that will cost you much more.

In addition to programmers and graphic designers, you will need team members who can handle other technical issues such as analyzing statistics, marketing your apps, setting up systems, and performing administrative work. Have an accountant and a lawyer on hand, too.

A fully scaled app team has eight positions: programmer, graphic designer, project manager, marketing manager, data analyst, technical assistant, accountant, and lawyer. Depending on your needs and your team members' skills, you could have one person covering several positions when you're scaling up. As you grow, you might need several people for each position.

1. Programmer

   The role and importance of programmers has been discussed in detail in Chapter 5. They will create your apps and initially be your entire team. When it comes to programmers, have several on call so not everything comes to a halt when a programmer becomes unavailable.

2. Graphic Designer

   In Chapter 5, we also discussed graphic designers. They will create the visual components of your apps and your marketing materials. You want them to be part of your programmer's development team. They can be independent contractors but development will be much smoother if the programmer and graphic designer are under one roof.

3. Project Manager

   Project managers play the most critical role on your team. They will manage everybody else and report back to you. They have to be versatile and be able to handle all parts of the business. They need to understand your vision and communicate with your team members to ensure the moving pieces are heading toward your vision. When you get started, you will be the project manager, but I suggest you find somebody for this role as soon as possible and when financially feasible. This will allow you to focus on the company's direction while the project manager is handling daily operations.

Once I started making money, I decided to bring in my friend who was running his own app business and gave him 10 percent of the company. He was the one who told me to get into the app business in the first place so it seemed like a good fit. He became an integral part of the team, and we doubled and then tripled our income. We did so well that we started two more companies together, which became equally successful. I would not recommend giving away 10 percent of your company unless you're 100 percent sure that person will bring extreme value.

4. Marketing Manager

Marketing managers should be current with all marketing tools and tactics to get your apps more downloads. These people constantly check the market, learn what strategies work, and implement them. They collaborate with data analysts to see how your app network is performing and create tweaks. These managers will write marketing copy and suggest changes that increase the app's traffic and sales conversions. This is a critical position because things are always changing, and the marketing manager has to stay current.

In my business, this is my role. I don't outsource it because it is my strength. One of the reasons for my success is that I check the market every day and adapt quickly. If you don't do this job, hire a high-level person who has proven himself or herself in the app marketing business.

5. Data Analyst

The data analyst's primary job is to collect and assess every piece of data your business is generating. This includes downloads, sales, user analytics, app rankings, and so on. This person constantly looks at all of your data and is responsible for helping the marketing manager determine what areas need improvement. You want someone who can look at the numbers, see the trends, and give advice.

6. Technical Assistant (TA)

A TA helps with daily technical tasks. These include submitting app updates, testing apps, and changing app names, nag screens, and promo pages. This is a vital role because the technical assistant is in the trenches. He or she ensures all of the project manager's orders are executed quickly and correctly. The TA needs to be available at all times. This person needs to be tech savvy and meticulous. There is no room for error here since something as simple as a mis-pointed nag screen can cost you several hundred dollars a day.

7. Accountant

You must have an accountant on your team. She pays all my bills and balances my accounts. I approve the payments, but I don't deal with paying anyone, and that frees up my time to work on something else. She pays the taxes, monitors my accounts, and gives me tax advice. She looks at the overall business budget and the budget for individual apps to see if expenses are where they should be.

Your accountant is an independent contractor and will work for you on an as-needed basis. Spend some time finding the right one because the accountant is critical to your financial success.

8. Attorney

You need a seasoned attorney on your team to create the nondisclosure and contractor agreements that all of your subcontractors will sign. The documents you sign with your independent contractors will protect your intellectual property. In most cases, you can use standard agreements, but you should still have your attorney examine them. Find an attorney who has expertise with technology and start-ups.

REMOTE MANAGEMENT

Once you move away from the old-school mindset of having employees under one roof, you will feel comfortable managing your team from anywhere, even far-flung places, like Fiji or Chile. Online project management sites like Basecamp (appempire.com/basecamphq) will help you coordinate with all members of your team. Everyone can be working on the same project from multiple locations around the world.

Your programmer and technical assistant need not meet in person. Online tools like Skype and Basecamp allow you and members of your team to communicate and coordinate any time to get the task done.

I manage all my employees from my iPhone. With the Basecamp app, I can see what my team members are doing, and how far along they are for any given projects. I can communicate what needs to be done and let them handle their work while I am planning my next adventure.

OUTSOURCING YOUR LIFE

While you're optimizing and automating your business, don't forget to do the same with your personal life. We do many things on a daily basis that we could outsource. Once you get to a certain level, it will make little sense for you to handle things like booking your hotels and flights, answering calls, and buying groceries. Many people think they have to be rich to have a personal assistant, but this is false. You can free much of your time without spending much money.

Imagine having somebody who helps you out 20 hours a week for $15 per hour. That's $300 a week or $1,200 a month, which will buy you an extra 80 hours a month. You can use that extra time to spend time with you family, go on a new adventure, or execute a plan to double your income.

I wanted to free up more time and take my lifestyle to the next level. So, I hired Kate, or Super Kate, as I call her. She used to be a personal assistant for A-List Hollywood actors and actresses. Now I have someone to answer calls, check my mail, set up my transportation, find the physical therapists I need for my arm, and so on. Super Kate allows me to spend more time in the zone, doing the things that I want to do. I am more productive, happier, and more fulfilled.

If it's time to take your lifestyle to the next level and, if you have the money, hire yourself a Super Kate. Even if you get somebody for a few hours a week, do it. You will be happy you did.

THE SEVEN PILLARS OF AN APP BUSINESS

You can outsource almost everything in your business besides the businessowner role. You will always need to maintain a bird's-eye view of your business at every stage of growth. Even though others might steer at times, you have only one captain per ship and your responsibility is to plot the course and ensure everything stays on track.

The key to monitoring your business while letting your team handle most of the action is to consistently focus on and check in on seven key areas. I call these the seven pillars of the app business:

1. Psychology and a Winning Mindset
2. Market Research
3. App Development and Maintenance
4. Analytics and Tweaking
5. Marketing and Monetization
6. Team and Systems
7. Professional Networking

I check in on these key areas every day. Even if I don't take action in every area, this reminds me of what I need to focus on. I've created specific questions for each one of these areas and reading these consistently puts me in a resourceful state and gives me new ideas to implement. Here is a brief recap for each area and the questions that you should answer on a regular basis. You can use these as an initial guide and add your own as you see fit.

1. *Psychology and a Winning Mindset.* A winning mindset is vital because this is where everything starts. If you don't have a vision, don't feel passionate about what you do, and do not have the flexibility and tenacity to adapt to the market, then you will have trouble focusing and maintaining the energy to make your business a long-term success.

Questions to Ask Yourself

- What is my vision for this company, and am I moving toward it?
- Why do I want to be successful in the app business? Who else will benefit from it?
- Is my attitude consistently positive and resourceful? How can I reinforce it?
- What can I do to strengthen my mind, body, or spirit more?
- Am I aligning myself with positive people who share my passion?
- Am I flexible and willing to change as the app business does?
- Do I believe I can make this work, or am I sabotaging myself by second-guessing my actions?

2. *Market Research.* The app store is your market, and like any market, it dictates how you need to run your business. The store fluctuates constantly, and you must monitor it so you can adapt to these changes quickly and seamlessly. Unlike most markets, it runs globally 24 hours a day, 7 days a week, with no downtime.

Questions to Ask Yourself

- What's working in the Top 200 app charts? Which apps are making money?
- What are other developers doing that I can emulate with my apps?
- What new apps can I develop?
- What are the long-term business trends?

- Read online articles and blogs to discover:
  - o What are current market trends?
  - o What are top app developers discussing?
  - o How can I take advantage of the new phone hardware or software?

3. *App Development and Maintenance.* You always need to have one or more new apps in the development pipeline. You need to tweak your existing apps. This allows you to increase the traffic of your app network and to sustain and increase your income.

Questions to Ask Yourself

- Do I have a new app in development?
- How long is it going to take to get new apps out? How can I accelerate the process?
- How can I improve my current apps?
- Am I investing enough revenue in my new and existing apps?
- Can I use some existing code to create new apps more quickly?

4. *Analytics and Tweaking.* Monitoring your analytics will allow you to make informed decisions about your business's direction. Analytics give critical feedback about the performance of your apps and your app network. Keeping track of this information and responding to it is vital to your success.

Questions to Ask Yourself

- How can I automate the tracking of my numbers?
- What numbers should I be tracking?
- How are my apps doing, and what can I tweak to increase sales?
- What are the results of my previous tweaks?
- Are my app rankings going up or down? Why?
- Are my downloads going up or down? Why?
- Are my sales going up or down? Why?
- Can I use the feedback in my reviews to improve my apps?
- How can I improve my apps to appeal to more users?

5. *Marketing and Monetization.* Effective marketing of your apps is as important as their development. Consistently tweak and improve your

marketing efforts. Always look for ways to generate the most amount of money from the traffic you have. Mastering marketing and monetization is a must if you want to make a lot of money with apps and keep the money coming for years.

Questions to Ask Yourself

- Am I using all known strategies to monetize my apps?
- Am I looking for new ways to monetize my apps?
- Are my marketing materials translated? What other languages can I translate to?
- Am I using affiliate links in my apps?
- How can I further improve my apps' icons, titles, descriptions, screen-shots, keywords, and categories?
- Are my nag screens and promo pages set up, and are they pointing to the right apps?
- How can I add in-app purchases?
- How can I increase ad revenue?
- What can I do to increase traffic more and grow my app network?
- How can I get other developers to cross-promote with me?

6. *Team and Systems.* You must have a well-trained team in place. It will help you execute quickly and free up your time so you can focus on key business areas. Surround yourself with positive and intelligent people and take full advantage of technology to systemize as much of your business as possible.

Questions to Ask Yourself

- Has my business reached a point where I need to add another team member?
- What role do I need to fill?
- Where can I find the best talent?
- Am I delegating and managing my team?
- How are my team members performing?
- Do I need to fire any of my team members?
- How well are my online collaboration tools working?
- What else can I automate in my business?
- Am I a positive role model for my team and inspiring it to improve?

7. *Professional Networking.* Networking within the app community creates an environment where you and other appreneurs can learn from each other. When you're part of a network, you will learn much faster and grow your business more easily. Other appreneurs can infuse new and lucrative ideas into your business, and you can do the same for them. It's beneficial to be part of a community that you share similar interests and aspirations with.

Questions to Ask Yourself

- Have I checked in with my developer network recently?
- How can I help other appreneurs?
- What do I want to ask my appreneuer network?
- How can I meet other appreneurs?
- What online app communities can I plug into?
- What app industry conferences, meet-up groups, or workshops can I attend?
- How else can I grow my developer network?
- Am I growing my mastermind group?

YOUR DAILY ROUTINE

The best way to check in with the seven pillars of your business is to create a daily routine you can follow. I developed my routine when I was recovering from my accident. To this day, I lie in bed every morning and review my analytics from my iPhone. I use this time to research the market to see what's working.

In addition to tracking metrics and doing market research, I spend some time making a list of things I want to get done for the day. I pass on my tweaks to my project manager, and let my team execute them. I check in on the progress throughout the day and see if the team has any questions.

I use unplanned "net-time" to check in with these pivotal areas. By that I mean I use free time throughout the day to check my apps and my team, like when I'm waiting in line somewhere, when I'm traveling, or when I have other idle time that would be unproductive. I use these brief moments to look at the market and take pulse of what's happening with my business.

This may seem a bit counterintuitive at first. Many people are used to working or playing for extended periods of time. The faster you can adapt this more free-flowing work style, the sooner you can enjoy the appreneur lifestyle.

Your routine can differ from mine, but turn it into a habit like brushing your teeth every morning so you don't have to think about it. You do it, and your business keeps humming along while you are enjoying life.

What I Learned

1.

2.

3.

Actions to Take

1. Decide to be dispensable.
2. Hire team members and scale your team as necessary.
3. Set up online systems to manage your team remotely.
4. Hire a Super Kate and outsource your life.
5. Check in on the seven pillars of your app business on a daily basis.
6. Create a daily routine for your business.

Afterword
JUMP!

After attending an event in Southern California, I overheard two people talking about California's Route 1 and how breathtaking the narrow rustic road was that hugged the coastline.

With my app business on cruise control, I rented a silver Mustang convertible to drive up the coast from Long Beach to San Francisco. I invited my friend Nella, who was at the event, to join me, since she had never experienced the famous coastline drive either. As we enjoyed the bright blue sky and wide-open road, we grooved to the radio, and laughed like kids with no worries in the world.

Rounding a bend on a narrow cliff road, I saw a random sign that said, "Skydiving. Take a right."

Nella didn't see the sign because she was busy playing her extraordinary air guitar, so I took advantage of the moment and turned right, heading down the gravel road. Above us, small planes were rising and dipping slowly. Ahead, a field opened into a sketchy looking airport that seemed desolate.

Nella asked with a nervous tone, "Where are we going?"

I looked at her and said, "We're going skydiving."

"What?" she asked.

"Yeah. It's go time, Iceman," I said.

Thirty minutes later, with parachutes attached, we were on a small plane, climbing higher into the open sky. Adrenaline was coursing through my veins as I looked down through the open airplane door. The Pacific Ocean was vast and seemed unforgiving. We climbed to an altitude of 10,000 feet, and instead of relaxing and turning on the approved electronic devices, it was time to jump.

Nella was up first. She was understandably scared and was clinging to the opening of the plane but was quickly repositioned by her jumping instructor. As the wind sucked them out of the plane, her screams made every hair on my body stand up on end. I was anxious yet exhilarated to let go.

"JUUUUUUMP!!"

As I dropped uncontrollably through the air, I realized that asking the instructor, who was attached to me, to do multiple flips might not have been the best idea. My stomach flew up to my throat, and it never returned.

As soon as I pulled the parachute, the screeching air that had been rearranging my face came to a halt and then: complete silence. My tense muscles released, and I was floating, seemingly weightless. The view was incredible. I could see the exotic redwood trees along the coast, the magnificent rippling light blue ocean, and the strip of beach where we were going to land. It felt as if time stood still. I became overwhelmed with gratitude for everything I had in my life, and it brought me to tears.

In some ways, I parallel this jump to my jump into the app business. It's scary at first when you are about to do something you've never done before. That first step out of the plane seems unimaginable. You muster all your strength, will power, and faith. You have an overwhelming angst that wants to pull you back and keep you safe. You can talk yourself out of taking that first step and let the opportunity of a lifetime pass you by.

But this time, for you, needs to be different.

This time *has* to be different.

Let this book serve as your parachute as you embark on your journey to fulfill your dreams and enjoy the lifestyle you've always wanted. Yes, things will be scary when you jump. They always are. You will be challenged, and it might feel as if you are free falling for a little while. But when everything comes together and your chute opens, your life will be different forever.

Apps were my vehicle to freedom, but there are countless other opportunities. If apps are not for you, find something that is. Don't settle for what is going on with your life, if it's not what you want it to be. Pick something else, and take action. The life you are meant to live is closer than you think. Don't hesitate. It's time.

It's time to jump.

Resources

WEBSITE

www.AppEmpire.com
Chadmureta.com (to follow the author)
App Empire App, iTunes—www.AppEmpire.com/theapp

MARKET NEWS AND RESEARCH

Mashable—www.AppEmpire.com/mashable
Chomp Analytics—www.AppEmpire.com/chomp
148Apps—www.AppEmpire.com/148apps
Gartner—www.AppEmpire.com/gartner
Electronista—www.AppEmpire.com/electronista
Mobile Entertainment—www.AppEmpire.com/mobile-ent

Appcelerator—www.AppEmpire.com/appcelerator

iLounge—www.AppEmpire.com/ilounge

HELP GUIDES AND TUTORIALS

Analytics and Management

AppFigures—www.AppEmpire.com/appfigures

AppViz 2—www.AppEmpire.com/appviz2

Top App Charts—www.AppEmpire.com/topappcharts

App Annie—www.AppEmpire.com/appannie

Position App, iTunes—www.AppEmpire.com/positionapp

BaseCampHQ—www.AppEmpire.com/basecamphq

Flurry Analytics—www.AppEmpire.com/flurry

Affiliate Marketing

Linkshare—www.AppEmpire.com/linkshare

TradeDoubler—www.AppEmpire.com/tradedoubler

DGM Pro—www.AppEmpire.com/dgmpro

Banner Advertising

AdWhirl—www.AppEmpire.com/adwhirl

AdMob—www.AppEmpire.com/admob

Millennial Media—www.AppEmpire.com/milmed

iAd—www.AppEmpire.com/iads

Networking

Apple Developer Forums—www.AppEmpire.com/appledevfor

Android Developer Forums—www.AppEmpire.com/androiddevfor

Windows Mobile Development Forums—
www.AppEmpire.com/windowsdevfor

Blackberry Support Community—www.AppEmpire.com/blackberrydevfor

Meetup—www.AppEmpire.com/meetup

TOP MOBILE APP DEVELOPMENT OUTSOURCING SITES

oDesk—www.AppEmpire.com/odesk

Elance—www.AppEmpire.com/elance

Guru—www.AppEmpire.com/guru

Freelancer—www.AppEmpire.com/freelancer

vWorker—www.AppEmpire.com/vworker

Get A Coder—www.AppEmpire.com/getacoder

Sourceingline—www. AppEmpire.com/sourcingline

DEVELOPER PLATFORMS

Apple iOS—www.AppEmpire.com/ios

Android—www.AppEmpire.com/android

BlackBerry—www.AppEmpire.com/blackberry

Windows—www.AppEmpire.com/windows

Acknowledgments

To friends and family (you know who you are) who never gave up on me and have showered me with praise and support, allowing me to be the person I am today. I stand here because of you, and I will never forget that.

To Anthony Robbins and Tim Ferris, you have inspired me and unleashed a man with a mission that will carry on a movement to benefit the world. Thank you. You are my true heroes.

Special thanks to Tayfun Karadeniz aka TK, aka TNutz. Without you, none of this would have been possible. Thank you for giving me the opportunity to have the life I have today. We are brothers from other mothers, and it has been an honor to be your business partner. We have many more battlefields to conquer, and I can say there is no one else I'd rather have by my side.

To Kate James, aka Super Kate, for being the glue that has held everything together. Thanks for being a rock star and for dealing with my nomadic, chaotic tendencies.

To my mother, Charlene Dindo, who, at every stage, has been by my side in full support. Thank you for caring and protecting me from the world. I am proud to be your son, and this light will continue to shine bright in honor of you.

To Robert Dindo. Without your faith in me and your $1,800 to get me started in this business venture, my dream life would have only been a figment of my imagination. I am thankful for you, and all your support; you were there when times were tough, and I'll never forget that.

To Alan Johanson. I'm glad I picked up the phone when you called. You are a pioneer, and I owe a lot of my success to your genius. Thank you for being a great teacher and always being available when this newbie appreneur had tons of questions. I tip my hat to you, my friend.

To Josh Goodine. Your ability to drink coffee and stay up all night, to get things done is unmatched. Empire Apps wouldn't have reached the heights it did if it weren't for your hard work and dedication. You are an absolute genius and a great friend, and I will always have your back.

To Lora Johnson. You have contributed more than you'll ever know. From sending me the iPod, to the beginning stages of the first app, you have been part of the magic, and I am forever thankful for your support, patience, and sacrifice.

To Shorty Vincent. You always find a way to conjure words of wisdom that ignite and inspire my soul. The world is a better place because of you, and I feel lucky to know you. Namaste.

To Shannon Vargo and Elana Schulman, thank you for your patience and confidence in the dream of a first-time author. You'll have the manuscript next Friday, I promise. ☺

To Helen Chang for your editing brilliance and incredible cheerleading. Any person who has the privilege to work with you is very lucky.

Last but not least, to everyone who was patient in this journey, and all the relationships that took a backseat for the vision and purpose of this book. Thank you. I feel like the luckiest guy in the world to have such selfless people like you in my life.

About the Author

Over the past decade, Chad Mureta's professional and personal lives have impacted each other in profound and unexpected ways. In 2009, a devastating car accident confined him to a hospital bed, where Chad discovered the possibilities of the emerging app market while experimenting with his iPhone. During that time, Chad realized that his real estate business was not only consuming his life, it was also in no way connected to what he was passionate about.

Without any tech experience, he developed an idea for a mobile application called "Fingerprint Security Pro," that would go on to be a bestseller in the App Store and serve as the catalyst for a new company, career, and way of life. Chad realized that through mobile apps, he could create a system that worked while he didn't. Now almost three years later, he has spearheaded the development and marketing of 46 apps, which have been downloaded over 35 million times worldwide.

While Chad loves the exciting nature of the app business, it's his true passion for living a life free from the 9-to-5 grind that propels him as an appreneur. By letting technology work for him, Chad has been living his bucket list: traveling the world, learning salsa, becoming a certified scuba diver and skydiver, and his list continues to grow every year. Chad uses the app business as a means to work less and truly "have a life."

As an author, speaker, consultant, and entrepreneur, Chad Mureta's unique insight, experience, and tenacity have enabled him to make his businesses thrive, all while living the life of his dreams and traveling the world.

Follow the author at chadmureta.com.

Index

Congratulations— You Made It!

Accept This As My Gift To You

Dear Apprenuer,

You're one step closer to your goals and to creating a lifestyle of absolute freedom. Since you've come this far, I know you're serious about creating your own App Empire and will take action immediately.

As with any new journey, there may be road blocks or unexpected setbacks. But don't worry. The book you hold in your hands, *App Empire*, is actually just a small part of a much bigger multimedia program which you can access right now absolutely free.

Enjoy your free multimedia experience at www.AppEmpire.com/ bonus!

—Chad